Listening · Speaking · Reading · Writing

An Integrated Skills Course for ESL Learners

CONNECTED

STUDENT BOOK

2

PAGODA Books

CONNECTED 2

Copyright © 2016 by PAGODA Books

All rights reserved. No part of this publication may be reproduced, stored in a retrieval system, or transmitted in any form or by any means, electronic, mechanical, photocopying, recording or otherwise, without the prior written permission of the copyright holder and the publisher.

Published by PAGODA Books
PAGODA Books is the professional language publishing company of the PAGODA Education Group.
19F, PAGODA Tower, 419, Gangnam-daero,
Seocho-gu, Seoul, 06614, Rep. of KOREA
www.pagodabook.com

First Published 2016
Twelfth Impression 2024
Printed in the Republic of Korea

ISBN 978-89-6281-703-4 (13740)

Publisher | Kyung-Sil Park
Writer | PAGODA Language Education Center

Introduction

CONNECTED series is a four-level course designed for college students who want to use English effectively in their daily lives. This course gives students the opportunity to build up communicative skills through step-by-step learning and practice in each section of every unit. It also provides students with online practice related to the student book and online exercises for TOEIC preparation. Students will learn the four main skills of listening, speaking, reading, and writing in addition to grammar and vocabulary.

There are 12 units in each book, and each unit consists of the following sections:

VOCABULARY

Vocabulary presents general, core, and authentic words and useful expressions in diverse ways. It stimulates students' interest in the theme of the unit. The practices and activities enable students to become familiar with the new words and their proper use.

CONVERSATION

Conversation introduces various real-life conversations among native speakers of English. These sections present key vocabularies used in natural settings allowing students to figure out the meanings using context clues. The conversations should be taken as a starting point for further conversations and help lead the class into further discussions. While some of the language has been simplified, the feeling and flavor of the conversation is kept authentic.

GRAMMAR

Grammar introduces essential grammar points to enhance appropriate grammar use and to ensure accuracy. Grammar practices followed by the presentation of grammar points enable students to understand the grammar rules better and advance their grammar skills. This helps students improve accuracy in their spoken and written communication.

READING

Reading passages present high-interest and contemporary topics in many kinds of genres, which are related to the unit theme. A pre-reading question introduces the topic of the reading passage allowing students to think about the topic. Students are also able to enhance their comprehension skills and understand the passages better through the reading comprehension questions followed by the reading passage.

LISTENING

The key to improving one's understanding and mastering a language begins with listening. This section contains diverse real conversations and presents them in a way that helps students understand native speakers. Most of the conversations are focused on the theme of the unit, but there is humor built into it, too. Recognizing and appreciating humor in a second language are just as important as learning the meaning of those dialogues.

SPEAKING

Speaking allows students to learn how to create variations in their speech and keep a conversation exciting. Students cannot express themselves in their own words by just memorizing vocabularies and typical expressions to respond to questions. The activities in this section enable students to practice a variety of language and to apply what they have learned in real-life situations. Language is never static. It is a dynamic dance that must be constantly moving in order to avoid that learned-by-rote feel.

READING SKILL

Reading Skill introduces essential reading skills that students need to develop to succeed in their academic reading. Basic reading skills, such as skimming, scanning, identifying topic sentences and supporting details, using context clues, making inferences, and various other reading skills are presented with practical exercises that help students build up their reading skills.

WRITING

Writing presents a diverse selection of topics to write about. Each writing topic is proceeded by warm-up questions that help students organize their ideas to develop stronger passages. Students are encouraged to review their peers' writings and revise their own writings based on the review from their peers. This will help students write more well-developed passages.

Book 2 Scope & Sequence

Unit	Topic	Vocabulary	Conversation	Grammar
01	He Is My Next-Door Neighbor p. 8	Relationships	I Had So Much Fun with Them	Simple Past
02	What Time Is the Party? p. 14	Celebrations	Happy Birthday!	Prepositions of Time
03	Which Season Do You Like the Best? p. 20	Seasonal Activities	Do You Like Spring?	Superlative Forms of Adjectives

Review Units 01~03 p. 26

Unit	Topic	Vocabulary	Conversation	Grammar
04	How Are You Going to Get There? p. 28	Transportation	How Do You Get There from Here?	Future with *be going to*
05	Do We Have Enough Food for Dinner? p. 34	Food	Let's Cook up Something Good!	Quantifiers
06	What Were You Doing Last Night? p. 40	Car Accidents	Call the Insurance Company	Past Progressive with Time Clauses

Review Units 04~06 p. 46

Unit	Topic	Vocabulary	Conversation	Grammar
07	I Never Have Anything to Wear p. 48	Frequency Expressions	What Am I Going to Wear?	Frequency Adverbs
08	I'd Like to Book a Flight p. 54	Booking a Flight	Here's Your Boarding Pass	Modal Verbs 1
09	What's the Special Today? p. 60	Restaurants	What's New on the Menu Today?	Modal Verbs 2

Review Units 07~09 p. 66

Unit	Topic	Vocabulary	Conversation	Grammar
10	What's the Matter? p. 68	Health Problems	Get Well Soon!	Modal Verbs 3
11	Did You Get My Text Message? p. 74	Telecommunications	Would You Help Me with This?	Causative Verbs
12	I'm Looking for the Student Union p. 80	College Campus	How Long Does It Take to Get There?	Questions with *How*

Review Units 10~12 p. 86

Reading & Reading Skill	Listening & Pronunciation	Speaking	Writing
• Doing Good Things for Others • Using Context Clues	• Spending Time with Family and Friends • Linking Consonants to Vowels	What Did You Use to Do?	What Did You Do Next?
• Groundhog Day History • Making Inferences	• Are You Ready for the Party? • Numbers	How Often Do You Do That?	Let the Festivities Begin!
• The Snowbirds – Traveling South in the Winter • Identifying the Topic and Main Idea	• Bundle up, It's Cold! • Sounds of Comparative and Superlative Suffix	Some Like It Hot, Some Like It Cold	That Was the Best / Worst Trip Ever!
• Bike Sharing System in Paris • Distinguishing Facts from Opinions	• We Should Try Something Different • Can and Can't	I Think We'll Be Going by Boat	What Are Your Holiday Plans?
• How to Make Chicken Breasts with Spinach and Cheese • Identifying the Topic and Main Idea	• Let's Go Grocery Shopping! • Vowel Sounds: [ai], [i] and [i:]	Should We Buy More Vegetables?	That Was the Strangest Food
• Car Accident and Car Crash • Finding Supporting Details	• May I See Your Driver's License? • Consonant Sounds: [t], [θ], and [ð]	What Happened to You?	Wow, That Hurts!
• Habits of Successful People • Using Context Clues	• I Always Drink Tea in the Afternoon • Stressing Frequency Adverbs	What Should I Wear?	I Always Take a Shower in the Morning
• A Paradise Island, Fiji • Making Inferences	• I'd Like to Make a Reservation • Reduced Sound of to and for	Are There Any Seats Available?	May I Have Time Off?
• The World's First Cafe in Venice • Cause and Effect	• Would You Mind If I Order First? • Blending of [w] and [ʊ]	What Would You Like to Have?	I Totally Recommend That You Go to That Restaurant!
• Unhealthy Effects of Smartphones • Summary	• Don't You Know That's Bad for You? • Reduced Sound of to	Are You Feeling Alright?	How Do You Keep Yourself So Healthy?
• New Film Casting • Identifying Pronoun References	• How Do You Communicate? • Distinguishing between L and R Sounds	Please, Check Your Messages	Do You Have Time to Meet on Monday?
• Campus Tour • Finding Supporting Details	• When Will It Be Ready? • Reduced -ing Sound	How Can I Go to the Chemistry Department?	Are you Looking for a Roommate?

UNIT 01

Vocabulary	Conversation	Grammar Point	Reading	Listen Up	Speaking Build-up
Relationships	I Had So Much Fun with Them	Simple Past	Doing Good Things for Others	Spending Time with Family and Friends	What Did You Use to Do?

He Is My Next-Door Neighbor

• Vocabulary • Relationships

 Online Practice

1. Listen and choose the correct word for each picture and write the letter. Unit 01_1

a. colleague	b. acquaintance	c. best friend	d. boss
e. boyfriend	f. relative	g. classmate	h. neighbor

1. Tony: _____

2. Paul: _____

3. Richard: _____

4. Nick: _____

5. Veronica: _____

6. Henry: _____

7. Timothy: _____

8. Jane: _____

2. Match each word with its definition.

1. acquaintance •   • a person you work with
2. colleague •   • a member of your family
3. relative •   • someone you know, but not very well

 **Pair Work**

Practice this dialogue replacing the underlined words.

> A: Who's this in the picture?
> B: This is <u>Bradley</u>. He's one of my <u>relatives</u>.

8   CONNECTED 2

Conversation • I Had So Much Fun with Them

1. Look at the picture and describe what is happening.

2. Listen to the conversation and fill in the blanks.

Thom: Wow! Where did you take this picture?

Laura: Oh, I went to Europe with my _____.

Thom: Really? I went to see the Sistine Chapel two years ago.

Laura: I didn't get to see that, but my _____ did.

Thom: What about this picture?

Laura: My _____ and I went scuba diving in the Caribbean in July.

Thom: My _____ and I are planning to do that next year.

Laura: It will be fun. Ah, here is my favorite picture!

Pair Work

Practice this dialogue replacing the underlined words.

A: What did you do during your last vacation?
B: I went to Jeju Island with my friends. It was very nice.

Grammar Point • Simple Past

Statements		Questions	
Affirmative	**Negative**	**Yes-No Questions**	**Wh-questions**
She **was** in Japan.	She **wasn't** in Japan.	**Was** she in Japan?	**Where was** she?
I **ate** fish.	I **didn't eat** fish.	**Did** you **eat** fish?	**What did** you **eat**?
He **studied** English.	He **didn't study** English.	**Did** he **study** English?	**What did** he **study**?

1. Unscramble the words to complete sentences in simple past.

1. You / cards / play / . _____
2. I / a car / want / . _____
3. We / the game / lose / . _____
4. not / I / early / get up / . _____
5. not / Jeff and Linda / to school / ride a bike / . _____

2. Complete the chart by writing correct sentences in simple past.

Affirmative Statements	Negative Statements	Yes-No Questions	Wh-questions
The ship disappeared.			What disappeared?
	He didn't talk to you.		Who
		Was Amy depressed?	How
	She didn't teach math.		What
		Did they buy a cap?	What did they buy?

👥 Pair Work

Practice this dialogue replacing the underlined words.

A: Who did you <u>go to the party</u> with?
B: I <u>went to the party</u> with <u>my classmate, Kate</u>.

Reading • Doing Good Things for Others

1. Look at the picture. What do you think the passage is about?

DAILY NEWS
World · Business · Finance · Lifestyle · Travel · Sport · Weather

Issue: 240104 Est - 1965

Monday June 5th

Have you ever done any volunteer work? According to a study, volunteering makes our mind healthier and helps us live longer. People's Health Magazine conducted a survey on the effect of volunteerism among 3500 volunteers. And the result shows that doing volunteer work increases our physical and mental health. People who volunteer to help others are less likely to be depressed, and have a better sense of well-being. They also have a 22 percent reduced chance of dying in the next ten years.

Although volunteering is related to mental health as mentioned above, more reasons are needed to decide whether it is surely the cause. Biological and cultural issues and social resources are often connected with better health and well-being. Better health shouldn't be the only reason to start volunteering.

Then, what else is good about volunteering? Besides better health, we can get to know more people, release our stress while talking with them, have greater happiness through the good work we are doing, and more importantly, help the people who are in need, thus making the world a better place.

[Reading Skill: Using Context Clues] Go to Page 88.

2. Read the passage. Write *T* for true or *F* for false for each statement.

1. Volunteering has positive effects on our mental health. _____
2. Volunteers tend to be more depressed. _____
3. There are many benefits of volunteering. _____

Group Work

Discuss these questions in a group.

- Have you ever done any volunteer work?
- What kind of volunteer work did you do?

Listen Up • Spending Time with Family and Friends

1. Getting Ready
Listen and write the letter on the correct picture. Unit 01_3

1.
2.
3.
4.

2. Easy Listening
Listen to the dialogue and answer the questions. Unit 01_4

1. What reservation did the woman make last week?
   a. a flight reservation   b. a hotel reservation

2. What is the man going to pick up on his way home?
   a. his suit   b. his ticket

3. When is the man going to leave for his trip?
   a. tomorrow   b. this afternoon

3. Hard Rock
Listen to the dialogue and answer the questions. Unit 01_5

1. Where did William go after spending time with his girlfriend?
   a. his old high school   b. his relative's place

2. Who did William get into some mischief with?
   a. a few acquaintances of his best friend   b. his relatives

4. Pronunciation Linking Consonants to Vowels Unit 01_6
Listen and practice. Notice the sounds of the consonants linked with vowels in the sentences.

| Turn off the lamp. | Tell us to stand up. |
| Can I have it? | Forget about it! |

CONNECTED 2

• Speaking Build-up • What Did You Use to Do?

1. Study the expressions to talk about what you used to do.

A: You used to play the piano, didn't you?
B: Yes, I used to play it when I was young. But I quit. It was too difficult for me.
A: Difficult? That's what I like about the piano.
B: Oh, are you still learning it? You've been working on it for almost a year now.
A: Yes. Perfection takes time. I'm in no rush.
B: I used to think like that. Don't just give it up like I did.
A: I won't. Thanks.

A
- Did you use to *verb*...?
- Didn't you use to *verb*...?

B
- Yes, I did when I was young.
- Yes, I did, but I don't do that anymore.
- Yes, I did, but I quit *verb-ing*...

2. Write three things you used to do but stopped doing in the blank space.

Example:

I used to smoke, but now I don't.

1.
2.
3.

Pair Work Practice this dialogue using the three things you wrote above.

A: What did you use to do when you were younger?
B: I used to build model ships, but I don't do it anymore.

Culture Awareness — Planning ahead

It is very common among western companies and people to make plans ahead of time. They try to plan out events and activities as early as possible. It is not uncommon for them to start planning for the end of the year in January. These plans are often flexible and may change, but they serve as a guideline for what is coming up. This also allows other team members to know how much time they have left to complete their part of a project. So, why don't you plan ahead, too?

[Writing: What Did You Do Next?] Go to Page 89.

UNIT 02

Vocabulary	Conversation	Grammar Point	Reading	Listen Up	Speaking Build-up
Celebrations	Happy Birthday!	Prepositions of Time	Groundhog Day History	Are You Ready for the Party?	How Often Do You Do That?

What Time Is the Party?

• Vocabulary • Celebrations

Online Practice

1. Choose the correct word for each picture and write the letter.

a. birthday	**b.** Valentine's Day	**c.** Easter	**d.** St. Patrick's Day	**e.** wedding anniversary
f. Christmas	**g.** Parents' Day	**h.** Groundhog Day	**i.** Thanksgiving Day	**j.** New Year's Day

2. Match each word with its definition.

1. Valentine's Day •   • the first day of the year
2. birthday •   • a day to celebrate with your loved ones
3. New Year's Day •   • the anniversary of the date on which you were born

👥 Pair Work

Practice this dialogue replacing the underlined words.

> **A:** When is <u>Halloween</u>?
> **B:** <u>Halloween</u> is <u>the 31st of October</u>.

Conversation • Happy Birthday!

1. Look at the picture and describe what is happening.

2. Listen to the conversation and fill in the blanks.

Alice: Happy _____, Daehan!
Daehan: You remembered! Thank you so much.
Alice: Why wouldn't I remember?
Daehan: Last year, it was on _____. So, most of my friends forgot my birthday.
Alice: Really? Does your birthday usually fall on the same day as Easter?
Daehan: No, that was the second time Easter and my birthday were on the same day.
Alice: You're lucky. My birthday is always on a holiday.
Daehan: I know your birthday is in the winter. Is it on _____?
Alice: Nope, my birthday is on _____ day.

Pair Work

Ask and answer about dates of celebrations.

A: When is your birthday?
B: My birthday is on July 12th. When is yours?
A: Mine is on April 24th.

Grammar Point • Prepositions of Time

Prepositions	Uses	Examples
at	times holiday periods meal time	at 10 p.m. / 5:30 / noon / night / midnight at Easter / Chuseok / Christmas at breakfast / lunch / dinner (time)
on	days days + night / morning afternoon / evening dates	on Sunday / the weekend / New Year's Day on Wednesday morning / Sunday afternoon on the 26th of March / the 4th of September
in	general time of a day months seasons years decades (10 years) centuries (100 years) millennium (1000 years)	in the morning / the afternoon / the evening in June / October in spring / summer / fall(autumn) / winter in 1971 / 1995 / 2006 in the sixties / the 1790s / the late nineties in the 7th century / the 2nd century B.C in the first millennium A.D.
without prep.	next week / weekend / month / year / season / semester last night / week / weekend / month / year / season / semester	

1. Circle the correct words.

1. His birthday is (at / in) May.
2. I usually go to my parents' house (on / in) Christmas.
3. We eat turkey together (on / at) Thanksgiving Day.
4. The class starts at 9 a.m. (on / at) Monday morning.
5. I like to drink coffee (on / in) the morning and tea (at / in) the afternoon.

2. Complete the sentences with the correct prepositions: *at*, *on*, or *in*.

1. The weather in Seattle is usually wet and cold _____ February.
2. Lucy is arriving on April 22nd _____ 5'clock _____ the afternoon.
3. They often go to the south of France _____ summer.
4. They got married _____ 1994.
5. If you are out alone _____ night, it is usually better to get a taxi.

 Pair Work

Practice using prepositions of time replacing the underlined words.

A: When is <u>Christmas</u>?
B: It's on <u>December 25th</u>.

A: When did <u>the Christmas start</u>?
B: It <u>started in 1971</u>.

• Reading • Groundhog Day History

1. Have you ever heard of Groundhog Day? What do you think the day is about?

People in the United States and Canada celebrate Groundhog Day on February 2nd. It is only a North American tradition. It was created on an old superstition. On that day, a groundhog comes out from a hole after winter sleep to see if there is a shadow. If it sees the shadow on a sunny day, the groundhog predicts there will be cold weather for six more weeks and goes back to the hole. But if there isn't any shadow because of clouds, it believes spring is near and stays above ground. This forecast or foretelling is an important Groundhog Day tradition.

This forecast came from the European tradition of Candlemas. Europeans believed that a sunny Candlemas day would lead the winter to continue for another six weeks. And on February 2nd, Europeans used to celebrate the Virgin Mary. Gradually, the traditions at Candlemas had mixed with different traditional stories. The Germans added an animal – a hedgehog. If the hedgehog is scared by his shadow on Candlemas, it foretells that winter would continue for another six weeks. This belief came to America during the 18th century from German migrants and became known as Groundhog Day.

[Reading Skill: Making Inferences] Go to Page 90.

2. Read the passage and answer the following questions.

1. **Who celebrates Groundhog Day?**
   _____ celebrate Groundhog Day.

2. **When is Groundhog Day?**
   Groundhog Day is _____.

3. **What does a groundhog predict if there is a shadow on a sunny day?**
   The groundhog predicts there will be _____ for six more weeks and a _____.

👥 Group Work

Discuss these questions in a group.

- Is there any traditional day that is similar to Groundhog Day in your country?
- What do you usually do on that day?

Listen Up • Are You Ready for the Party?

1. Getting Ready Listen and match each celebration with its date.

1. My parent's wedding anniversary •
2. Julius's house warming party •
3. Easter •
4. Halloween •

• a. October 31st
• b. at the end of March
• c. November 12th
• d. July 22nd

2. Easy Listening Listen to the dialogue and answer the questions.

1. What kind of party are the man and woman going to attend?
   a. a Halloween party
   b. a housewarming party

2. When does the party start?
   a. at 9 o'clock
   b. at 10 o'clock

3. What is Freddie's costume supposed to be?
   a. Frankenstein
   b. Dracula

3. Hard Rock Listen to the dialogue and answer the questions.

1. Which celebration did the man forget?
   a. his girlfriend's birthday
   b. his one-year anniversary with his girlfriend

2. What does the man need to do?
   a. make a dinner reservation
   b. buy flowers

4. Pronunciation Numbers

Listen and practice. Notice the differences in the sounds of -teen [ti:n], -teenth [ti:nθ], -ty [ti] and -tieth [tiəθ].

13 [θɜr'ti:n]	—	13th [θɜr'ti:nθ]	30 ['θɜrti]	—	30th ['θɜrtiəθ]
14 ['fɔr'ti:n]	—	14th ['fɔr'ti:nθ]	40 ['fɔrti]	—	40th ['fɔrtiəθ]
15 ['fɪf'ti:n]	—	15th ['fɪf'ti:nθ]	50 ['fɪfti]	—	50th ['fɪftiəθ]

• Speaking Build-up • How Often Do You Do That?

1. Study the expressions to talk about how often you do something.

A: Your house looks great!
B: Thanks! It's decorated for the upcoming holidays.
A: How often do you change the decorations?
B: I usually change them for the different seasons.
A: Wow, that must be hard to do.
B: Not really. It doesn't take much time.
A: Don't you have to clean your house often, too?
B: I just clean it every two weeks.
A: Really? I feel I have to clean my house every other day.

A
- Do you change decorations frequently?
- How many times a year do you do that?

B
- I decorate it for every holiday.
- I change them once a season.
- Sometimes I do it once a week / twice a week / once every two weeks / once in a while.

2. Fill in your answers about how often you do the activities. Use the frequency expressions given.

Frequency Expressions	
once a day	twice a day
once a week	twice a week
once a month	twice a month
once a year	twice a year
almost never	never

Activities	You	Your partner
go to a party		
eat out for dinner		
read a book		
hang out with friends		
do online shopping		
go on a trip		

 Pair Work Ask and answer about how often you do the activities in the chart above. Complete the chart with your partner's answers.

A: How often do you read a book?   B: I read a book once a month.

Culture Awareness — Everyman's Birthday

In some countries of the world, everyone turns one year older on the first day of the year. This is known as everyman's birthday. This often leads to confusion for westerners. In many western countries, they count their age by the number of times they have celebrated their birthdays. Until a child has seen his or her second anniversary of their birth, their age is usually counted in months; three months old, nine months old, 18 months old, etc. For example, If you were born on March 17, 2000, you would become two years old on January 1st, 2001 for everyman's birthday. However, the child would be nine months old in the west, and wouldn't turn one-year-old until his birthday on March 17, 2001.

[Writing: Let the Festivities Begin!] Go to Page 91.

UNIT 03

Vocabulary	Conversation	Grammar Point	Reading	Listen Up	Speaking Build-up
Seasonal Activities	Do You Like Spring?	Superlative Forms of Adjectives	The Snowbirds –Traveling South in the Winter	Bundle up, It's Cold!	Some Like It Hot, Some Like It Cold

Which Season Do You Like the Best?

• Vocabulary • Seasonal Activities

 Online Practice

1. Choose the correct word for each picture and write the letter.

> **a.** go on a picnic   **b.** plant trees   **c.** go surfing   **d.** go water-skiing   **e.** fly a kite
> **f.** go sunbathing   **g.** pick fruit   **h.** build a snowman   **i.** go snowboarding

2. Fill in the blanks using the correct words from the box above.

1. Finally, it's autumn. We can _____ from the trees.
2. We _____ on Arbor Day in spring. It's April 5th in Korea.
3. In winter, kids like to _____ on a snowy day.

👥 Pair Work

Ask and answer about your favorite seasonal activities.

> **A:** What is your favorite thing to do in <u>spring</u>?
> **B:** I like to <u>go on a picnic</u>.

20 CONNECTED 2

Conversation • Do You Like Spring?

1. Look at the picture and describe what is happening.

2. Listen to the conversation and fill in the blanks.

Doug: Annie, would you like to _____ tomorrow?
Annie: Sounds like fun.
Doug: I know a great place near the lake.
Annie: Hum… Should I bring my bathing suit?
Doug: Sure, we could do some _____, or maybe even _____.
Annie: Oh, I love waterskiing. But I've lost my bathing suit.
Doug: Umm… Okay, then I have the best idea. Why don't we _____?
Annie: No, I don't like those small kites.
Doug: I was thinking of the bigger ones.
Annie: Well, while you are flying your kite, I'll just _____.

Pair Work

Ask and answer about your favorite seasons.

A: What is your favorite season?
B: My favorite season is fall. I love the beautiful fall foliage.

Grammar Point • Superlative Forms of Adjectives

Rules		Examples	
one-syllable adjectives	wild + est – wildest	late bright	→ the latest → the brightest
one-syllable adjectives ending in a vowel + a consonant	wet + t + est – wettest	big hot	→ the biggest → the hottest
two-syllable adjectives ending in -y	lazy (y → i) + est – laziest	happy early	→ the happiest → the earliest
all other two or more syllable adjectives	most + amazing – the most amazing	expensive → unusual	the most expensive → the most unusual
irregular forms	–	good bad far	→ the best → the worst → the farthest
two-syllable adjectives that take either -est or most	quiet → the quietest → the most quiet simple → the simplest → the most simple friendly → the friendliest → the most friendly		

1. Circle the correct superlative forms of the adjectives.

1. Who is the (tall / tallest / taller) person in your family?
2. My mother is the (best / good / better) cook in the world.
3. December is the (coldest / cold / most cold) month of the year in my country.
4. What's the (dangerous / most dangerous / dangeroust) animal in the world?
5. Ethan is the (most happy / happiest / happy) boy that I know.

2. Complete the sentences with the correct superlatives.

1. My house is _____ (big) in my neighborhood.
2. This flower is _____ (beautiful) in the world.
3. This is _____ (interesting) book I have ever read.
4. He is _____ (clever) boy in the town.
5. Malibu is _____ (peaceful) in the Pacific Ocean.

 Pair Work

Practice using superlative forms of adjectives replacing the underlined words.

A: What is the largest country in the world?
B: Russia is the largest.

• Reading • **The Snowbirds – Traveling South in the Winter**

1. Look at the picture. What do you think the passage will talk about?

Snowbirds are people from the U.S. Northeast, U.S. Midwest, Pacific Northwest, or Canada. They are usually seniors. They spend most of the winter in warmer places, and they return to family and friends in the summer so that they can avoid the snow and cold weather in northern areas.

Some of them have their own businesses. They have a second home in a warmer place, or their business can be moved easily like a flea market to meet sellers. Some snowbirds move their homes with campers or boats along the east coast.

Florida has been the most popular site for the snowbirds. Other southern cities also have some places for snowbirds to enjoy the warm climate. Many snowbirds tend to choose vacation places where they can pay low or no income tax.

[Reading Skill: Identifying the Topic and Main Idea] Go to Page 92.

2. Read the passage and answer the following questions.

1. What is a snowbird?
   a. a person who lives in northern areas and spends winter in warmer places
   b. a person who lives in southern areas and spends winter in warmer places
   c. a person who lives in northern areas and spends summer in warmer places
   d. a person who lives in northern areas and spends winter in cold places

2. Where is the best snowbird site?
   a. Canada   b. Florida   c. U.S. Northeast   d. Pacific Northwest

3. Where do most snowbirds choose their vacation places?
   Their vacation places are _____.

Group Work

Discuss these questions in a group.
- Where do you want to spend your summer and winter?
- What would you like to do there?

Listen Up • Bundle up, It's Cold!

1. Getting Ready Match each activity with the best season to do it.

1. building a snowman
2. picnicking under the cherry blossoms
3. sunbathing
4. snowball fighting
5. waterskiing
6. raking leaves

a. spring
b. summer
c. autumn
d. winter

2. Easy Listening Listen to the dialogue and answer the questions.

1. What are the man and woman talking about?
   a. what to do on a snowy day   b. how to build a snowman

2. What does the woman say about skiing?
   a. It is not as hard as snowboarding.   b. It is harder than snowboarding.

3. What does the man want to do outside?
   a. go snowboarding   b. build a snowman

3. Hard Rock Listen to the dialogue and answer the questions.

1. What does the woman want to look at?
   a. the Moon   b. Jupiter

2. What does the woman remind the man to bring?
   a. a coat and gloves   b. some coffee and hot cocoa

4. Pronunciation Sounds of Comparative and Superlative Suffix

Listen and practice. Notice how the comparative and superlative suffixes are pronounced.

tall - tall**er** - tall**est**	large - larg**er** - larg**est**
short - short**er** - short**est**	gentle - gentl**er** - gentl**est**

24 CONNECTED 2

Speaking Build-up • Some Like It Hot, Some Like It Cold

1. Study the expressions to talk about your favorite season.

   A: What is your favorite season?
   B: I like fall best.
   A: What do you like to do in the fall?
   B: I love hiking in the mountains.
   A: So do you like it better when it is cool?
   B: It's much better than the summer. I hate the hot weather.

   A
   - What's your favorite time of year?
   - When is the best time of year?
   - Which season do you like best?

   B
   - My favorite time is fall.
   - The best time is when the leaves are turning colors.
   - Fall is the best season for me.

2. Fill in the chart with three things you like to do in each season.

Winter	It is fun to catch snowflakes on my tongue in winter.	Spring 	I like to collect flowers and press them in a book.
Summer 	I like to swim in the ocean.	Fall/Autumn	Fall is the perfect season to go hiking on the mountain.

Pair Work
Practice the dialogue in Part 1 using the sentences you wrote above.

Culture Awareness — British English vs. American English

Both countries use English as their first language. Even though they both speak English, there are some differences that have been developed between the two dialects over the last two hundred years. Some of them are pronunciation and different terms.

* Americans say: fall   – elevator – apartment – subway   – restroom – garbage
  British people say: autumn – lift   – flat   – underground – toilet   – rubbish

[Writing: That Was the Best / Worst Trip Ever!] Go to Page 93.

Review Units 01~03

• Conversation • What Are Your Plans for the Holiday?

1. Listen to the conversation and fill in the blanks.

   Laura: Hey, Doug. Do you have any plans for your _____ holiday?
   Doug: Annie and I are planning to visit my _____ and her _____.
   Laura: Wow, that sounds like a lot of traveling.
   Doug: It is, but it's always good to go home. How about your plans?
   Laura: Well, my boyfriend and I are going to celebrate our one year anniversary.
   Doug: Has it been a year already?
   Laura: Yep. We met on the field day.
   Doug: I forgot that you went to school together.
   Laura: Yes, we did. And I'm _____ for us after the actual holiday.
   Doug: Aren't you going to visit your hometown?
   Laura: I can't. I have to work at my part-time job.
   Doug: Oh, no! Didn't your _____ give you the day off?
   Laura: No, but that's okay. I'm making extra money for Daehan's present.

2. Make plans for a special event. Fill in the chart by making a note of the place, the time, the food, the activities, etc.

Occasion	New Year's Eve party	
Date and Time	December 31, at 8 p.m.	
Location	my apartment	
Guests	boss, colleagues, best friends, spouses of colleagues	
Foods & Drinks	potluck party (Each person brings one dish to share with everyone.) BYOB (Bring Your Own Beverage)	
Activities	dancing, icebreaker games, talking, and socializing	

 Pair Work Take turns asking and answering about the plans you made above. Use the following questions.

- What kind of events are you planning?
- When is it going to be?
- Where is it going to be?
- Who is invited?
- What foods and drinks will be served?
- What activities are you planning to do?

Reading • Family & Alumni Summer Parties

Read the passage and choose the best answer to each question.

College of William & Mary Family Summer Parties will be held on Jun 22nd at the second oldest college in the nation.

This party is a fun way for new students to meet and mingle with current students, alumni, and their families. It is also a great time to catch up during the summer. The alumni and current students give advice to incoming students, offer them anecdotes, and share campus experiences for the younger or incoming students. This will help the new students prepare for College of William & Mary and get their energy level up about post-campus adventures. They can also have a chance to see one of the most beautiful campuses in the world. They will love the buildings on campus consist of Georgian and Anglo-Dutch architecture. It is the highlight to take a photo in front of Christopher Wren building, the oldest collegiate building in the United States.

This event is hosted by the boosters and current students of the school. The boosters include volunteer students, alumni, and their parents. For those interested in helping to plan future events, there is a sign-up section on the website in the Parents & Families or Alumni pages. You can also visit the site to check out the photos from these fun-filled events from the past. Future parties and details will be available from the College of William & Mary calendar, so be sure to check back often, especially in the late spring.

- **Date:** Jun 22nd
- **Party Time:** 18:30 - 22:30
  Campus tour starts at 16:30 at Kimball Theater
- **Venue:** One Tribe Place
- **Campus:** 116 Jamestown Road, Williamsburg
- **Contact:** Stephanie Tapply 757-221-4596
- **Party Registration:** Tickets are available

1. **What is the story mainly about?**
   a. a campus tour for new students
   b. the most beautiful campuses in the world
   c. college summer parties
   d. current students and alumni meeting

2. **What do the most buildings of the college consist of?**
   a. Georgian and Anglo-Dutch architecture
   b. Georgian and Romanesque architecture
   c. Gothic and Anglo-Dutch architecture
   d. Baroque and Georgian architecture

3. **Where are the new students going to take a picture?**
   a. in front of Christopher Wren building
   b. in front of Kimball Theater
   c. in front of Historic Triangle
   d. in front of the Williamsburg area

4. **What should students do if they are interested in becoming a future host?**
   a. They should visit the information center.
   b. They should go to the volunteer sign-up section in Alumni building.
   c. They should come to the Family Summer Party.
   d. They should visit the volunteer sign-up section on Parents & Families or Alumni pages.

5. **Where will the further party details be available?**

UNIT 04

Vocabulary	Conversation	Grammar Point	Reading	Listen Up	Speaking Build-up
Transportation	How Do You Get There from Here?	Future with *be going to*	Bike Sharing System in Paris	We Should Try Something Different	I Think We'll Be Going by Boat

How Are You Going to Get There?

• Vocabulary • Transportation

Online Practice

1. Choose the correct word for each picture and write the letter.

a. taxi	b. subway	c. sports car	d. SUV	e. limousine	f. van
g. express bus	h. maglev train (magnetic levitation train)			i. ferry	j. truck

2. Fill in the blanks using the correct words from the box above.

1. An _____ is a powerful vehicle with four-wheel drive that can be driven over rough ground. It is an abbreviation for sport utility vehicle.

2. It takes about 15 minutes to get from Shanghai Airport to Pudong by _____. It is moved by high performance magnets.

3. A _____ is a boat that can carry people and cars at the same time.

Pair Work

Practice this dialogue replacing the underlined words.

A: How do you go to <u>school</u>?   B: <u>I go to school by subway</u>.

28 CONNECTED 2

• Conversation • **How Do You Get There from Here?**  Online Practice

UNIT 04

1. Look at the picture and describe what is happening.

2. Listen to the conversation and fill in the blanks. Unit 04_1

Alex: How are you going to go home for Thanksgiving?
Mary: I have a ticket for a _____ at seven tonight.
Alex: I heard that there is going to be a snowstorm later today. You may want to change to the _____ like I did.
Mary: Oh, no! A snowstorm could cancel all the flights.
Alex: You should come with me on the train most of the way.
Mary: Most of the way? Then what?
Alex: We can rent a _____ or take a _____.
Mary: Renting a car sounds better than taking a bus.
Alex: Call the _____ and cancel your ticket first. Then later, I'll call a _____ to go to the train station.

Pair Work

Ask and answer about what kind of transportation you would take to get to a place.

A: How are you going to go <u>home for the holiday</u>?
B: I'm going to <u>take the bus</u>.

Unit 04 How Are You Going to Get There? 29

Grammar Point • Future with *be going to*

 Online Practice

Form: *am / is / are* + *going to* + verb

Statements		Questions	
Affirmative	**Negative**	**Yes-No questions**	**Wh-questions**
I **am going to** study.	*I* **am not going to** study.	**Am** *I* **going to** study?	**Who is** *going to* study?
You/We/They **are going to** study.	*You/We/They* **are not going to** study.	**Are** *you/we/they* **going to** study?	**What are** *you* **going to** study?
			When are *we* **going to** study?
			Where are *they* **going to** study?
He/She **is going to** study.	*He/She* **is not going to** study.	**Is** *he/she* **going to** study?	**How is** *he* **going to** study?
			Why is *she* **going to** study?

1. Complete the sentences using *be going to*.

1. **A:** Where are you going? **B:** I _____ visit a customer.
2. **A:** Do you want me to help you? **B:** No thanks. John _____ help me.
3. She's already decided. She _____ buy a new car.
4. _____ you _____ go shopping today?

2. Choose the correct answers.

1. **A:** Where is she going to spend her vacation?
   B: She _____ spend her vacation in Hawaii.
   a. is going to   b. are going to   c. was going to   d. will going to

2. **A:** When are we going to meet for the rehearsal?
   B: We _____ meet at 6 p.m.
   a. is going to   b. are going to   c. am going to   d. will going to

3. **A:** Who is going to make John's birthday cake?
   B: I _____ make it.
   a. is going to   b. are going to   c. am going to   d. will going to

 Pair Work

Practice asking and answering questions using *be going to*.

A: What are you going to do?   **B:** I'm going to get a driver's license.

Reading • Bike Sharing System in Paris

1. Look at the pictures. What do you think the passage will talk about?

There are many great cities to be a cyclist, but some cities are truly bicyclists' paradise. The top 20 cities are Amsterdam, Copenhagen, Utrecht, Seville, Bordeaux, Nantes, Antwerp, Eindhoven, Malmö, Berlin, Dublin, Tokyo, Munich, Montreal, Nagoya, Rio de Janeiro, Barcelona, Budapest, Paris, and Hamburg. They are scored by 13 factors, including cycling facilities, culture, sharing programs, gender balance, policies, and traffic safety. The names of cities start from number 1 to 14 because there are a few ties. Paris is ranked 13th. The bike sharing system of Paris is called Vélib. It is all over the city and is the best way to see Paris.

Go to a bike stand and find a green bike and check the tires and brakes. Then you can borrow the bike. You can ride the bike for free for the first 30 minutes. After the 30 minutes, an extra charge is added every 30 minutes: 1€ for the first half an hour and 2€ for the second. After the third extra 30 minutes, 4€ is charged every 30 minutes. When you return the bike, you can insert the Vélib in the locking mechanism at any free bike stand in the city.

[Reading Skill: Distinguishing Facts from Opinions] Go to Page 94.

2. Read the passage and answer the following questions.

   1. What is the passage mainly about?
   - a. a bike sharing system of Paris
   - b. great cities for cyclists
   - c. the way to use Vélib
   - d. the top 20 cities of cycling

   2. What is NOT true about the top 20 bicyclists' paradise?
   - a. They include Amsterdam, Copenhagen, Utrecht, Seville, Bordeaux, and Nantes.
   - b. They include Tokyo, Munich, Rio de Janeiro, Barcelona, Budapest, Paris, and Hamburg.
   - c. They are scored by 15 factors.
   - d. Paris is ranked 13th.

   3. Which is true about the payment system for renting a bike in Paris?
   - a. You don't have to pay for the first 30 minutes.
   - b. You will pay 2€ for the first extra 30 minutes.
   - c. You will pay 1€ for the second extra 30 minutes.
   - d. You will pay 1€ per half hour after the third additional 30 minutes.

👥 Group Work

Discuss these questions in a group.

- Have you ever traveled by bike?
- If you had a chance to travel by bike, where would you like to go?

• Listen Up • **We Should Try Something Different**

1. Getting Ready Listen and match each person with the transportation he or she is going to take.

1. Marcus •
2. Elizabeth •
3. Catherine •
4. Daniel •

• **a.** train
• **b.** bus
• **c.** airplane
• **d.** limousine

2. Easy Listening Listen to the dialogue and answer the questions.

1. What tickets are offered for free next week?
   a. the maglev train tickets **b.** round-trip train tickets

2. Why didn't the woman want the tickets at first?
   a. She doesn't have time. **b.** The trains are too noisy.

3. What is special about the maglev train?
   a. It floats on the water. **b.** It floats on magnets.

3. Hard Rock Listen to the dialogue and answer the questions.

1. What kind of transportation is the woman going to use first for the travel?
   a. a train **b.** an airplane

2. What happened to the woman three years ago?
   a. She was fined for speeding. **b.** She had some accidents.

4. Pronunciation *Can* and *Can't*

Listen and practice. Notice the reduced sound of *can* compared to the sound of *can't*. The stress falls on the verbs following *can*.

| I can drive a car. | He can sing. | They can play soccer. |
| I can't drive a car. | He can't sing. | They can't play soccer. |

32 CONNECTED 2

• Speaking Build-up • I Think We'll Be Going by Boat

1. Study the expressions to ask a person about how he or she is going to get to a place.

A: <u>How are you going to get to the show tonight?</u>
B: My friend and I are going to share a taxi.
A: Are you going any place after the show?
B: I think we're going to go to the after party.
A: And how are you going to get to the party?
B: We're going to take a bus.
A: Ok, I will be waiting for you.
B: Thanks.

A:
- How do you plan to get to …?
- How are you going to …?
- How are you going to get to …?

2. Fill in the chart by writing sentences about how you would travel to the following destinations.

	a tropical island	e.g.) I am going to take a cruise ship to a tropical island.
	a waterfall	
	a snow-covered mountain	
	an old castle	

Pair Work

Practice this dialogue using the chart above.

A: How are you going to travel to <u>the tropical island</u>? B: I am going to take <u>the cruise ship</u>.

Culture Awareness — Going Home for the Holidays

In America, Canada, and Australia, it can be difficult to travel back home. All three countries are very large, and travel can literally take days by car or bus. It's usually faster to travel by airplane. But some people don't like airplanes because they prefer not to have to go through security. Most airlines limit you to one bag with a weight restriction. Due to some of the difficulties and expense of travel, some people don't make it home for the holidays.

[Writing: What Are Your Holiday Plans?] Go to Page 95.

UNIT 05

| Vocabulary
Food | Conversation
Let's Cook up
Something Good! | Grammar Point
Quantifiers | Reading
How to Make Chicken Breasts
with Spinach and Cheese | Listen Up
Let's Go Grocery
Shopping! | Speaking Build-up
Should We Buy More
Vegetables? |

Do We Have Enough Food for Dinner?

• Vocabulary • Food

 Online Practice

1. Choose the correct word for each picture and write the letter.

a. celery	b. cabbage	c. wheat	d. oats	e. plum
f. beef	g. salmon	h. chicken	i. nuts	j. yogurt
k. cheese	l. butter	m. olive oil	n. grape	o. milk

Pair Work

Ask and answer about what you want to eat.

A: What would you like to eat?
B: I'd like a salad with salmon and nuts.

34 CONNECTED 2

• **Conversation** • **Let's Cook up Something Good!**

1. Look at the picture and describe what is happening.

2. Listen to the conversation and fill in the blanks.

Rick: Let's make stew. Do we have _____, onions, and _____?

Emily: Yes, but we need more.

Rick: Then I'll go buy some. What else do we have in the fridge?

Emily: We have _____, pork, and _____.

Rick: We can use the pork, but _____ always tastes better.

Emily: Okay. Do we need anything else?

Rick: We need some _____, a loaf of bread, and some _____.

Emily: Oh, some cheese and wine would be good, too.

Rick: Right, I will go to the store now.

Emily: Okay! See you when you get back.

Pair Work Practice this dialogue replacing the underlined words.

> **A:** Why don't we make <u>a sandwich</u>?
> **B:** Sure, but we don't have <u>any bread</u>.

Unit 05 Do We Have Enough Food for Dinner?

Grammar Point • Quantifiers

Online Practice

	Quantifiers			
Countable Nouns	many	a few	few	a lot of
Uncountable Nouns	much	a little	little	some / any

※ We usually use **some** in affirmative sentences and **any** in negative sentences and questions.
e.g.) I have **some** money. / I don't have **any** money. / Do you have **any** money?

1. Complete the sentences with the correct quantifiers: *a/an, some,* or *any*.

1. Are there _____ apples in the kitchen?
2. There are _____ people hanging out at the mall.
3. Is there _____ park in the middle of New York City?
4. **A:** These french fries are awful. There isn't a drop of ketchup on them.
   B: Well, there's _____ on the shelf in the kitchen.

2. Complete the sentences with the correct quantifiers: *little, a little, few, a few, many,* or *much*.

1. We must do this quickly. There is very _____ time.
2. Excuse me, may I ask _____ questions?
3. My hometown isn't very popular; very _____ people come to visit.
4. I don't think Angela would be a good mother. She has _____ patience.
5. There aren't _____ parks in the center of Oxford.
6. There isn't _____ milk left in the fridge.

Pair Work

Practice using quantifiers with countable and uncountable nouns.

A: Is there <u>any cheese</u> in the refrigerator?
B: Yes, there is <u>a little cheese</u> left.

• Reading • How to Make Chicken Breasts with Spinach and Cheese

1. Have you ever cooked your favorite dish? How do you cook the food?

Phytochemicals are found in plant-based foods such as fruits, vegetables, beans, and grains. It reduces the danger of certain kinds of cancer and other diseases. The dish, chicken breasts stuffed with spinach and cheese, has a phytochemical-rich filling, so it fights long-term illness and helps to protect your eyesight.

Ingredients
6 boneless, skinless chicken breast halves (about 700g)
3/4 teaspoon salt
1/4 teaspoon black pepper
1/2 teaspoon dried basil, powdered
1 box (300g) frozen green spinach, melted and squeezed dry
6 roasted red bell pepper halves
6 thin slices of low-fat or Swiss cheese (120g)
1/2 cup low-fat buttermilk
2 cups fresh whole-wheat bread crumbs

This is how to make chicken breasts with spinach and cheese. Put each chicken breast flat between plastic wrap to 3mm thickness. Season one side with salt, pepper, and basil. Add the other side with spinach, red pepper, and cheese dividing equally and leave 5mm empty from the edge. Roll up breasts around filling and close with toothpick. Dip each breast in buttermilk, and then coat lightly with crumbs. Place the chicken, joint side down, on baking sheet. Bake until the chicken is cooked through and crumb coating is browned after about 35 minutes. Remove toothpicks and serve.

[**Reading Skill:** Identifying the Topic and Main Idea] Go to Page 96.

2. Read the passage and answer the following questions.

1. Which is NOT one of the main ingredients?
   a. boneless, skinless chicken breast halves   b. frozen green spinach
   c. thin sliced low-fat or Swiss cheese   d. fat-free soy milk

2. What is NOT true about phytochemicals?
   a. It is found in plant-based foods.   b. It reduces the danger of certain kinds of diseases.
   c. It helps to protect your eyesight.   d. It fights short-term illness.

3. Which of the following is NOT a seasoning to make chicken breasts with spinach and cheese?
   a. salt   b. sugar   c. basil   d. pepper

Group Work

Discuss these questions in a group.
- What is your favorite dish to cook?
- Why is it your favorite?

• **Listen Up** • Let's Go Grocery Shopping!

1. Getting Ready
Listen and write the name of the person under the correct list.
Unit 05_2

Rachel

Cindy

Jerry

LIST 1
Cake Mix
10 Eggs
1ℓ Milk
Icing
Candles

LIST 2
1 loaf of Bread
1 package of Ham
1 bottle of Mustard
1 Head of Lettuce
1 Tomato

LIST 3
Vanilla Ice Cream
300g Cherries
Chocolate sauce
Packaged Sprinkles

1. _____   2. _____   3. _____

2. Easy Listening
Listen to the dialogue and answer the questions. Unit 05_3

1. What does the child want to buy?
   a. cookies
   b. carrots

2. Why doesn't the child like carrots?
   a. because they hurt her teeth
   b. because they hurt her braces

3. What does the mother ask the child to do?
   a. to get some carrots
   b. to get some milk

3. Hard Rock
Listen to the dialogue and answer the questions.
Unit 05_4

1. What kind of meat is the customer interested in buying?
   a. pork
   b. beef

2. What does the customer NOT ask the clerk about?
   a. where the diary products are
   b. how to cook beef stew

4. Pronunciation
Vowel Sounds: [aɪ], [ɪ], and [i:]
Unit 05_5

Listen and practice. Notice the differences in the sounds of [aɪ], [ɪ], and [i:].

[aɪ]	[ɪ]	[i:]
diner	dinner	dean
wine	milk	cheese

38 CONNECTED 2

• Speaking Build-up • Should We Buy More Vegetables?

1. Study the expressions to ask what to buy for groceries.

A: Would you look in the refrigerator for me?
B: Sure. What are you looking for?
A: <u>Do we have any eggs and milk?</u>
B: <u>We have eggs, but we don't have some milk</u>.
A: How about tomatoes and cheese?
B: We don't have any tomatoes. And the cheese is moldy.
A: Okay, would you like to go grocery shopping with me?
B: Why not? Can I get some chocolate?

A
- Do we need to buy some eggs and milk?
- Are there enough eggs or milk?
- Should we buy more eggs and milk?

B
- We should buy some more.
- We have enough for tonight.

2. Imagine that you are going to make the following three dishes. Make shopping lists to buy the ingredients for the dishes.

pasta	beef steak	apple pie
ground beef, tomatoes, garlic…		

👥 Pair Work

Ask and answer about the dish you are going to make using the shopping list above.

A: What ingredients do you need to cook <u>pasta</u>?
B: I need some <u>ground beef, eggs, and bread crumbs</u>.

Culture Awareness — Potluck Dinner

A good way to have a party and get other people to help make it is to have a potluck meal. Everyone must bring some food to the party. The food should be enough for several people to share. With a large group, people might be asked to bring a certain type of food; main dish, drinks, dessert, etc. Everyone places the food in one location, and a buffet style meal is ready.

[Writing: That Was the Strangest Food] Go to Page 97.

| UNIT 06 | Vocabulary
Car Accidents | Conversation
Call the Insurance Company | Grammar Point
Past Progressive with Time Clauses | Reading
Car Accident and Car Crash | Listen Up
May I See Your Driver's License? | Speaking Build-up
What Happened to You? |

What Were You Doing Last Night?

• Vocabulary • Car Accidents

1. Choose the correct word for each number and write the letter.

| a. tow truck | b. pile-up | c. hit and run |
| d. T-bone | e. head-on collision | f. bump each other |

1.
2.
3.
4.
5.
6.

 **Pair Work**

Practice this dialogue replacing the underlined words.

A: What happened over there?
B: There was <u>a pile-up</u>.

40   CONNECTED 2

Conversation • Call the Insurance Company

1. Look at the picture and describe what is happening.

2. Listen to the conversation and fill in the blanks.

Eileen: Oh, no! Were you in another _____?

Jerry: Well, yes. But this time, it wasn't my fault.

Eileen: Okay, what happened?

Jerry: I was driving on a highway and a car _____ mine.

Eileen: Didn't you see the driver?

Jerry: Yes, I did. He just didn't see me.

Eileen: How bad was the _____?

Jerry: Not bad. Just some _____ and _____, but he drove away before I could get out of my car.

Eileen: You mean a _____?

Jerry: Yes, so I called the police and the insurance company.

Pair Work

Practice this dialogue replacing the underlined words.

A: What happened to your car?   **B:** A truck bumped my car.

Unit 06 What Were You Doing Last Night? 41

Grammar Point • Past Progressive with Time Clauses

Past progressive with *while* clause	Past progressive with *when* clause	Simple past with *when* clause
• *While* I **was having** a shower, the phone rang. = I was in the middle of taking a shower when the phone rang. • Jessica **was singing** *while* I **was sleeping**. = Jessica was singing at the same time that I was sleeping.	• *When* she left home, you **were studying**. = You started studying before she left home. • *When* they arrived, Jeff **was cooking** dinner. = Jeff started cooking before they arrived.	• *When* she left home, you **studied**. = She left and then you studied. = You started studying after she left. • *When* they arrived, Jeff **cooked** dinner. = They arrived and then Jeff cooked. = Jeff started cooking after they arrived.

1. Complete the sentences with *when or while.*

1. What were you doing _____ you were waiting for me?
2. She was driving too fast _____ the light changed.
3. Sonia was watching TV _____ her parents got home.
4. The phone rang _____ we were eating dinner.
5. Tom and I were having coffee _____ he invited me to his party.
6. Were you listening to him _____ he was talking?

2. Complete the sentences with *before or after.*

1. We were walking to work when the fire broke out.
   = We started walking to work _____ the fire broke out.
2. It was raining when I woke up this morning.
   = It started raining _____ I woke up this morning.
3. I watched TV when my brother came back home.
   = I started to watch TV _____ my brother came back home.
4. She called us when we started Graham's birthday party.
   = She called us _____ we started Graham's birthday party.

 **Pair Work**

Practice this dialogue replacing the underlined words.

A: What were you doing <u>while the music was playing</u>? **B:** I <u>was dancing</u>.

Reading • Car Accident and Car Crash

1. Have you ever been in a car accident? Can you recall what happened?

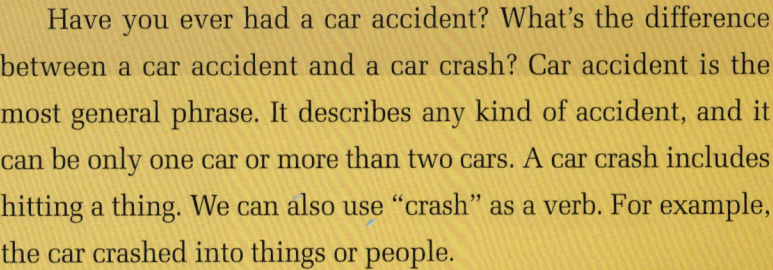

Have you ever had a car accident? What's the difference between a car accident and a car crash? Car accident is the most general phrase. It describes any kind of accident, and it can be only one car or more than two cars. A car crash includes hitting a thing. We can also use "crash" as a verb. For example, the car crashed into things or people.

When two cars crash into each other from the front, this is called head-on collision. This is one of the most dangerous kinds of accidents because people can be killed. The opposite kind of accident is a fender-bender. It is a small accident with slight damage to the cars. When several cars hit each other, we call it a pile-up. Pile-ups often occur when the weather and road conditions are bad. Sometimes a car hits a person, but the driver doesn't stop and drives away. This is called a hit and run.

Car accidents can be caused by a number of reasons and they can not only damage cars but also lead to killing people. Fatality is a more formal word for someone killed in an accident. When a car is seriously damaged and can't move, then it needs to be helped. Damaged cars can be towed and moved by another car. The helping car is called a tow truck.

[**Reading Skill:** Finding Supporting Details] Go to Page 98.

2. Read the passage and answer the following questions.

   1. What is it called when two cars crash into each other from the front? _____
   2. What is a pile-up? _____
   3. What is a more formal word for someone killed in an accident? _____

Group Work

Discuss these questions in a group.
- What do you usually do when you see a car accident?
- What would you do if you were in a car accident?

• Listen Up • **May I See Your Driver's License?**

1. **Getting Ready** Choose and write the correct word for each picture.

| speeding ticket | traffic jam | car scratch |

1. _____
2. _____
3. _____

2. **Easy Listening** Listen to the dialogue and answer the questions.

   1. Where did Rachel get hurt?
      a. her arm
      b. her chest

   2. What is the name of Rachel's cat?
      a. James
      b. Garfield

   3. Why was Rachel hurt?
      a. She was trying to give her cat a haircut.
      b. She was trying to bathe her cat.

3. **Hard Rock** Listen to the dialogue and answer the questions.

   1. What does the police officer ask the man to give him?
      a. his license and proof of insurance
      b. his proof of insurance

   2. How fast was the man going?
      a. 40 mph in a 30 mph zone
      b. 60 mph in a 30 mph zone

   *mph (miles per hour)

4. **Pronunciation** Consonant Sounds: [t], [θ], and [ð]
   Listen and practice. Notice the differences in the sounds of [t], [θ], and [ð].

[t]	[θ]	[ð]
tin	thin	this
mat	math	mother

• Speaking Build-up • What Happened to You?

1. Study the expressions to ask and answer about what happened.

A: Hey, what's the matter? You don't look well.
B: I'm okay. It's just my legs that hurt a little.
A: What happened?
B: I just missed a step in the dark and fell down a few stairs last night.
A: I'm sorry to hear that. But what were you doing these at the time?
B: I was trying to get a midnight snack.
A: Are you going to be all right?
B: Of course, it isn't as bad as it looks.

A
- What's wrong with you?
- Is everything alright?
- Are you all right?

B
- It's nothing / okay.
- Don't worry about it.
- You don't have to worry.

2. Look at the people in the pictures. Write down what you think probably happened to each of them.

Marianna	William	Annie

Pair Work Ask and answer questions using the chart above.

A: What do you think happened to Marianna?
B: Maybe she ate too much ice cream and had a stomachache.

Culture Awareness — Being Pulled over

In many countries around the world, the scariest thing that can happen when you are driving is being pulled over by a police officer. If you see flashing lights behind you, make your way to the side of the road and pull over. Roll down your window most of the way. Keep your hands on the steering wheel. Wait for the officer until he or she comes to your window. When he or she asks you for your driver's license and registration, tell the officer what you are going to do. "I am going to take my wallet out of my pocket." Move slowly. If you think the officer may not be real, you may ask to see his or her badge.

[Writing: Wow, That Hurts!] Go to Page 99.

Review Units 04~06

• Conversation • Tell Me What Happened!

1. Listen to the conversation and fill in the blanks.

Steve: Leigh, may I borrow your _____?
Leigh: Sorry, it has a flat tire. What happened to yours?
Steve: It had a _____ last night.
Leigh: _____?
Steve: Well, last night I went to get some _____ and _____ at a grocery store.
Leigh: I remember. We had cheeseburgers together with Del at your home last night.
Steve: Well, I locked up my bike downstairs like usual.
Leigh: Of course. What happened next?
Steve: When Del left, he must have put his car in reverse instead of drive.
Leigh: Oh no, did he run over your bike?
Steve: Yep, he caused some _____. Oh, well. I guess I'd better call a taxi to get to work.
Leigh: When Rick comes home, we'll take your bike in his truck to the repair shop.
Steve: Thanks.

2. Fill out the following accident report form.

Accident Report Form

Type of Vehicle
- ☑ Car/Automobile   ☐ Van/Bus   ☐ Truck
- ☐ Train   ☐ Motorcycle/Bicycle   ☐ Other

Describe Vehicle(s) _Black and white Sedan, License plate VBX 832_

Location of Accident
- ☑ Parking Lot   ☐ Highway   ☐ Street
- ☐ Driveway   ☐ Other

Specific Location _Parking lot of M-mart_

Type of Accident
- ☐ Rear-End Collision   ☐ Dent   ☐ T-Bone
- ☑ Hit and Run   ☐ Fender Bender   ☐ Other

Descriptiion _The car backed into mine and drove away very fast._

Accident Report Form

Type of Vehicle
- ☐ Car/Automobile   ☐ Van/Bus   ☐ Truck
- ☐ Train   ☐ Motorcycle/Bicycle   ☐ Other

Describe Vehicle(s) _____

Location of Accident
- ☐ Parking Lot   ☐ Highway   ☐ Street
- ☐ Driveway   ☐ Other

Specific Location _____

Type of Accident
- ☐ Rear-End Collision   ☐ Dent   ☐ T-Bone
- ☐ Hit and Run   ☐ Fender Bender   ☐ Other

Descriptiion _____

 Pair Work Role-play a conversation using the report form in Part 2 and the questions below.

Questions	Follow-up Questions
• What happened?	• Then what? What next?
• Where did the accident take place?	• Can you describe it?
• Who was involved?	• Do you know who saw the accident?

• Reading • Camping

Read the passage and choose the best answer to each question.

The Johnsons decided to spend time in the great outdoors. Mr. Johnson searched for good campsites online. He found some parks offering amenities like toilets, water pumps, and showers. Some were cleaner than others. Some parks were located by a lake and were good for fishing, but no hiking trails were available. A few of the campsites offered special activities such as rock climbing or kayaking. He chose the park in Arizona where they could go hiking and rock climbing, and he made a reservation on the website.

He asked his two sons to help him pack the camping equipment in one big storage tub. They put a tent, sleeping bags, sleeping pads, a first aid kit, lanterns, a flashlight, extra batteries, a small whisk broom, wet wipes, matches, a bug repellent, trash bags, and cooking supplies in it. Mrs. Johnson made sure they didn't forget anything before the trip such as sunscreen, a pocketknife, camp or lawn chairs, clothes, firewood (if needed), toothbrushes, a cooler, and food. She tried to avoid cooking elaborate meals. They were so excited to go camping.

The great thing about camping for them is that it is the most cost-effective way to get away from it all, and even a weekend can do wonders for their spirit.

1. **How did Mr. Johnson find a good campsite?**
   a. He searched on the Internet.
   b. He asked his friends.
   c. He read on a camping book.
   d. He paid a visit.

2. **Why did he choose the park in Arizona?**
   a. because they can go fishing
   b. because it has swimming pools and mini golf
   c. because it was cleaner
   d. because they can go hiking and rock climbing

3. **Which is NOT the item they put in the big storage tub?**
   a. a tent
   b. a lantern
   c. a cooler
   d. a bug repellent

4. **What did Mrs. Johnson check before the trip?**
   a. the stuff they keep in the big storage tub
   b. the things they need to pack right before the trip
   c. the campsite Mr. Johnson booked
   d. the things they need to bring back after the trip

5. **Why is the camping good for Johnson's family?**
   a. It's the most cost-effective way to get away from it all.
   b. It's good for their health.
   c. Kids love outdoor activities.
   d. It can do wonders for their work.

UNIT 07

Vocabulary Frequency Expressions | **Conversation** What Am I Going to Wear? | **Grammar Point** Frequency Adverbs | **Reading** Habits of Successful People | **Listen Up** I Always Drink Tea in the Afternoon | **Speaking Build-up** What Should I Wear?

I Never Have Anything to Wear

• Vocabulary • Frequency Expressions

1. Choose and write the correct word for each description.

twice a month

never

every few hours

once a year

several times a week

frequently

all the time

from time to time

rarely

1.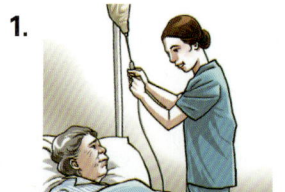
Mary is a nurse. She **often** works at night.

2.
Kelly is a student. She **sometimes** cooks.

3.
Sally is a Taekwondo coach. She **always** practices.

4.
Tom and Sue are teachers. They travel on summer vacation **every year**.

5.
Sarah and Peter practice dancing **every two weeks**.

6.
Ryan does **not** play sports **at all**. He enjoys reading.

7.
Terry reads books for his granddaughter **several times a day**.

8.
Tina and Rose **almost never** go swimming. They love cycling.

9.
Mike is a cook. He walks his dog at night **four times a week**. He missed it only once.

 Pair Work Practice asking and answering questions using frequency expressions.

A: Do you <u>cook from time to time</u>?
B: No, I <u>almost never cook</u>.

48 CONNECTED 2

• **Conversation** • **What Am I Going to Wear?**

1. Look at the picture and describe what is happening.

2. Listen to the conversation and fill in the blanks.

Shannon: What are you wearing on your date, Rachel?
Rachel: I don't know. I _____ have anything to wear.
Shannon: What about this red dress?
Rachel: Oh, I _____ wear that one to work.
Shannon: Well, how about this outfit? You _____ wear it.
Rachel: That outfit is so out of style. Ugh! Can I borrow some of your clothes?
Shannon: But I _____ get my things back from you.
Rachel: What do you mean? I _____ return your stuff.
Shannon: Really? What about this blue dress?
Rachel: Well, _____, I forget.

Pair Work

Ask and answer about how often you wear certain clothes.

A: How often do you wear that jacket?   **B:** I wear it several times a week.

• Grammar Point • Frequency Adverbs

Online Practice

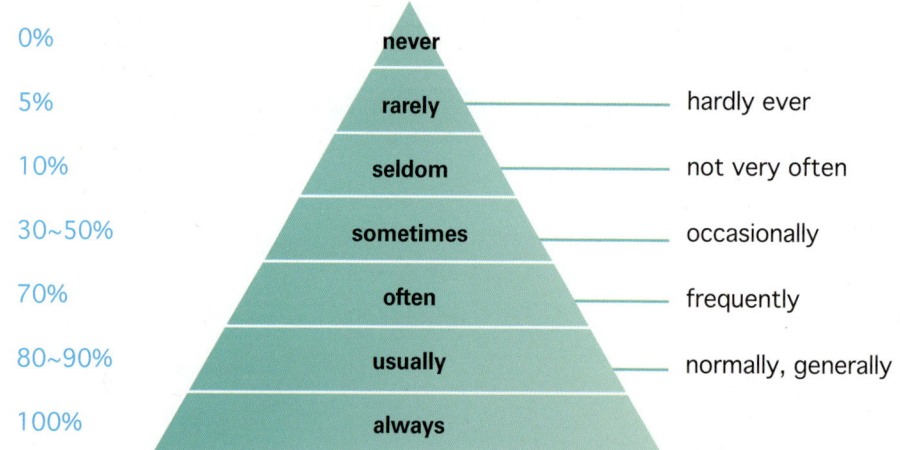

1. Complete the sentences with the correct frequency adverbs.

1. I _____ eat breakfast. — 80%
2. I _____ drink alcohol. — 5%
3. I _____ go to the cinema. — 70%
4. I _____ visit my grandmother. — 30%
5. I _____ watch TV. — 10%
6. I _____ jog in the morning. — 0%
7. I _____ go to bed before 11 p.m. — 100%

2. Choose the correct answers.

1. I drive to work almost every day.
   a. usually   b. sometimes   c. occasionally   d. hardly ever

2. Julia wears a hat and gloves three times a week.
   a. often   b. sometimes   c. rarely   d. never

3. They go hiking in the mountains once a year.
   a. always   b. normally   c. occasionally   d. rarely

Pair Work Practice this dialogue replacing the underlined words.

A: How often do you exercise?
B: I frequently exercise.

Reading • Habits of Successful People

1. Do you have any habits that need to be changed? How do you think you can change those habits?

Stephen Covey wrote the world famous self-help book, *The Seven Habits of Highly Effective People*. His best-known book was published in 1989 and has sold more than 25 million copies. He is supporting values with so-called "universal and timeless" principles. In his book, he shows how a person or a group can become successful and offers practical ways to make it come true.

In the first section, he suggests three habits to help people change from dependence to independence. Among the three, the first habit is to be positive. This is to help improve roles and relationships in life. The second habit is to begin with the end in mind and to set priorities for success.

And the final habit mentioned in the book is to sharpen the saw. It is a continuous development in both personal and interpersonal influence. Having good health, reading more books, and maintaining a responsible lifestyle are important to renew yourself.

[**Reading Skill:** Using Context Clues] Go to Page 100.

2. Read the passage and answer the following questions.

1. What is the title of the world famous self-help book written by Stephen Covey?

2. What is the final habit he suggests?

3. Choose the correct answers.

1. What is the second habit suggested in the book?
   - **a.** to be positive
   - **b.** to think creatively
   - **c.** to understand others
   - **d.** to begin with the end in mind

2. What is NOT mentioned about renewing yourself?
   - **a.** having good health
   - **b.** listening to music
   - **c.** reading more books
   - **d.** maintaining a responsible lifestyle

Group Work

Discuss these questions in a group.

- What habits do you practice to be more successful in life?
- What habits should you practice to become healthier?

• Listen Up • I Always Drink Tea in the Afternoon

1. Getting Ready Listen and write the correct frequency words under the pictures: *always*, *usually*, *sometimes*, or *rarely*.

Laura	John	Daniel	Alice

2. Easy Listening Listen to the dialogue and answer the questions.

1. Why does the woman ask the man, "What's happening?"
   - a. The man looks tired.
   - b. The man looks sad.

2. What does the man do when he isn't working?
   - a. He sleeps.
   - b. He enjoys his free time.

3. Why is the man working so hard?
   - a. to save money
   - b. to pay off his loans and credit card bills

3. Hard Rock Listen to the dialogue and answer the questions.

1. Why are the baseball players wearing armbands?
   - a. to raise money
   - b. to promote their games

2. How much will the man and the woman donate?
   - a. $55
   - b. $65

4. Pronunciation Stressing Frequency Adverbs
Listen and practice. Notice how the frequency adverbs are stressed in the sentences.

He always works late.	They often take a walk after dinner.
I usually eat lunch at noon.	She never does her homework.
We rarely see him.	Occasionally they succeed.

52 CONNECTED 2

• Speaking Build-up • What Should I Wear?

1. Study the expressions to talk about what to wear.

   A: What are you doing?
   B: I have a date with Jill tonight. But all the clothes are dirty.
   A: How about wearing this?
   B: Ugh, smell it. I have to get that cleaned.
   A: Well, when is your date?
   B: It's in two hours.
   A: How about spraying it with some deodorizer?
   B: Does that work?
   A: It does on TV. Let's try it.

   B
   - I don't know what to wear.
   - I have nothing to wear.
   - What should I wear?

   A
   - Why don't you wear this?
   - How about that? Don't you like it?

2. Fill in what kind of clothes you would wear for each of the following occasions.

a job interview		hanging out with friends
male	**female**	
suit dress shirt necktie black socks black shoes	suit blouse stockings heels	

a sports event	a social event

Pair Work Practice this dialogue using the chart above.

   A: What are you going to wear to your interview on Thursday?
   B: I think I will wear my black suit, a white blouse, and low-heel black shoes.

Culture Awareness — The Trap

There are questions people ask when there is no way to answer. The old question, "Does this make me look fat?" is a classic example. This is what is called a loaded question. If you answer, "No, it doesn't." then the questioner will think they must look fat all the time. If you answer, "Yes, it does." Then the questioner will think that you are insensitive. Please be careful to ask or answer one of these questions.

[Writing: I Always Take a Shower in the Morning] Go to Page 101.

UNIT 08 I'd Like to Book a Flight

Vocabulary: Booking a Flight | Conversation: Here's Your Boarding Pass | Grammar Point: Modal Verbs 1 | Reading: A Paradise Island, Fiji | Listen Up: I'd Like to Make a Reservation | Speaking Build-up: Are There Any Seats Available?

• Vocabulary • Booking a Flight

1. Choose the correct word for each number and write the letter.

a. boarding pass
b. economy class
c. passport
d. luggage
e. aisle seat
f. arrival and departure board
g. customs officer
h. security checkpoint

1. ____
2. ____
3. ____
4. ____
5. ____
6. ____
7. ____
8. ____

2. Fill in the blanks with the correct words from the box above.

Agent: May I have your _____, please?
Kyle: Here you go.
Agent: Are you checking in any _____?
Kyle: Just this one.
Agent: OK, please place your luggage on the scale. Here is your _____ for economy class.
Kyle: Thanks.

Pair Work

Practice this dialogue about booking a flight replacing the underlined word.

A: Do you have any seats available to go to <u>LA</u>?
B: Yes, would you like a window or an aisle seat?

54 CONNECTED 2

• Conversation • Here's Your Boarding Pass

1. Look at the picture and describe what is happening.

2. Listen to the conversation and fill in the blanks.

Kara: May I see your airline ticket, sir?

Paul: Sure, here you are.

Kara: Thank you. You will be in seat 33C in _____.

Paul: Is that an _____?

Kara: Yes, it is also an exit row seat. Here is your _____.

Paul: Thank you.

Kara: Excuse me, sir. May I see your _____?

Paul: Is there a problem?

Kara: It's too large for the overhead bins. Your _____ must be checked in.

Paul: Alright, but please waive the baggage fee.

 **Pair Work**

Practice this dialogue replacing the underlined words.

A: Do you have any baggage to check in? **B:** Yes, I'd like to check in one suitcase.

• Grammar Point • Modal Verbs 1

Modals	Uses	Examples
can	ability	I **can** ride a bike.
	request / permission	**Can** you do this for me? / **Can** I borrow your pen?
	possibility	Smoking **can** cause lung problems.
could	ability in the past	When I was younger, I **could** climb trees.
	request / polite permission	**Could** you help? / **Could** I bother you for a second?
	possibility (less possible than *may* or *might*)	I **could** wait for you, but I'm not sure.
may	permission	**May** I use your bathroom?
	possibility	I **may** go to New Zealand next year.
might	polite permission	**Might** I suggest we send it tomorrow?
	possibility	It **might** snow later.

1. Choose the correct modals.

1. I _____ speak Russian fluently when I was living in Moscow. Now, I _____ only say a few phrases in the language.
   - **a.** could - can
   - **b.** can - could
   - **c.** could - could
   - **d.** can - can

2. As the teacher said, we _____ read this book for our own pleasure only in class.
   - **a.** may
   - **b.** couldn't
   - **c.** could
   - **d.** might

3. **A:** _____ you stand on your head for more than a minute? **B:** No, I _____.
   - **a.** Couldn't - can
   - **b.** Can't - can
   - **c.** Can - can't
   - **d.** Couldn't - can't

4. Take an umbrella. It _____ rain later.
   - **a.** might
   - **b.** can't
   - **c.** could
   - **d.** might not

5. _____ I ask a question?
   - **a.** Must
   - **b.** May
   - **c.** Will
   - **d.** Would

2. Complete the sentences with the correct modals: *can, can't, could, couldn't,* or *may*.

1. I _____ move the table. It was too heavy.
2. _____ you open the window, please?
3. I'm afraid I _____ play tennis tomorrow. I've got a dentist appointment.
4. I'm so hungry I _____ eat a horse!
5. His excuse _____ be true, but I don't believe it.

Pair Work Practice using modal verbs replacing the underlined words.

A: <u>May</u> I <u>have your passport</u>, please?   **B:** Here you go.

• Reading • **A Paradise Island, Fiji**

1. Think about which tropical island is best for vacation.

Fiji is in the middle of the South Pacific. It is called the heart of the South Pacific and a real paradise with 333 beautiful tropical islands. Travelers love white sandy beaches, tall coconut trees, pristine oceans, and many waterways to explore. People relax on shining white beaches at sunset. They can snorkel, dive, surf, or kayak in the perfect oceans. They can also enjoy whitewater rafting on clear and clean waterways and cruise around the mainland and outer Fiji Islands. Trekking rainforests, backpacking the outer islands, visiting welcoming villages, and experiencing living in unique culture and history can add enjoyment.

If they want to experience the city, they can check out Nadi. Nadi is full of excitement with crowded streets, attractive shops, and wonderful dining. In the Yasawa Islands, they can enjoy exceptional natural beauty. There aren't any shops, medical centers, banks, or cafes. There are only great beaches and sunshine. Vanua Levu is Fiji's second largest island. They can see beautiful sites like untouched rainforest with hiking trails. Suva is the capital city of Fiji. It's the largest city in Oceania. Kadavu is one of the best places to experience true Fijian culture. There are a lot more islands they should visit in Fiji. Fiji is a dream of a lifetime, and travelers can make many beautiful memories.

[**Reading Skill:** Making Inferences] Go to Page 102.

2. Read the passage and answer the questions.

1. Where is Fiji? _____
2. What is the largest city in Oceania? _____

3. Choose the correct answers.

1. **Which is NOT true about Fiji?**
   a. There are sandy beaches, rainforests, and cities.   b. It is a big tropical island.
   c. Travelers can also experience the city life in Fiji.   d. Travelers can enjoy many outdoor activities.

2. **Where is one of the best places to experience the true Fijian culture?**
   a. Levu   b. Kadavu   c. Yasawa   d. Nadi

Group Work

Discuss these questions in a group.

- Have you ever traveled abroad?
- Where is the best place you've visited?

• Listen Up • I'd Like to Make a Reservation

1. **Getting Ready** Listen and fill in the blank spaces based on the people's travel plans.

Names	Where	When	How
Christina			airplane
Fredrick		July 3rd	
Peter	Milan		

2. **Easy Listening** Listen to the dialogue and answer the questions.

   1. How many travel packages is the travel agent offering?
      a. one
      b. two

   2. What kind of upgrades are available for the five-day package?
      a. a sauna trip, a king size bed, and a room upgrade
      b. a sauna trip, a queen size bed, and a room with a view

   3. How many days are in the simple package?
      a. four days
      b. five days

3. **Hard Rock** Listen to the dialogue and answer the questions.

   1. Which flight does the man prefer taking?
      a. a non-stop flight
      b. a flight with a layover

   2. How long does it usually take to get through security?
      a. an hour
      b. thirty minutes

4. **Pronunciation** Reduced Sound of *to* and *for*
   Listen and practice. Notice the reduced sounds of *to* and *for*.

To whom is this going? [tu]	This is going to my house. [tə]
What are you looking for? [fɔr]	This is for you. [fər]

58 CONNECTED 2

Speaking Build-up • Are There Any Seats Available?

1. Study the expressions for making a flight reservation.

A: Five Star Airlines. How may I help you?
B: Hi. I'd like to book a flight to Chicago this Friday.
A: Could I have your name first, please?
B: It's Charles Dickens.
A: We have flights at ten in the morning and five in the afternoon.
B: Morning flight sounds good.
A: Okay. Would you prefer business or economy class?
B: Economy, please.
A: Alright, Mr. Dickens. You're all set.
B: Thank you.

B
- I'd like to make a reservation for a flight to Chicago this Friday.
- Do you have any seats available to Chicago on Friday?

A
- Which would you prefer: business or economy class?
- Would you like business or economy class?

2. Imagine you're planning to go on a trip. Fill in your answers to the questions.

	e.g.) Mark	You
Where are you going?	Beijing and Shanghai in China	
How long will your trip be?	2 weeks	
When does your trip start?	January 15	
How do you want to get there? Do you have any preferences?	by plane to Beijing, by train to Shanghai, and back home by plane	
Are you traveling alone or with a companion?	with my girlfriend	
Will you need a hotel or car reservation?	hotel reservations	

Pair Work Take turns asking and answering about your plans for the trip using your answers above.

A: Where would you like to go on a trip?
B: I'd like to go to China.

A: How are you going to get to China?
B: I'm planning to take a plane.

Culture Awareness — Traveler's Etiquette

Be aware of your surroundings. When you travel, always be aware that there are people around you. They may or may not speak the same languages as you, but try to remember that not everyone needs to hear your conversation. Some people consider it the height of rudeness to have a loud conversation in a crowded space. There are always people around you and they may be listening.

[Writing: May I Have Time Off?] Go to Page 103.

UNIT 09	Vocabulary Restaurants	Conversation What's New on the Menu Today?	Grammar Point Modal Verbs 2	Reading The World's First Cafe in Venice	Listen Up Would You Mind If I Order First?	Speaking Build-up What Would You Like to Have?

What's the Special Today?

• Vocabulary • Restaurants

 Online Practice

1. Choose the correct word for each number and write the letter.

a. vegan option	b. today's special sign	c. beverage	d. starter	e. menu
f. main dish	g. reservation sign	h. side dish	i. dessert	j. cutlery

1.
2.
3.
4.
5.
6.
7.
8.
9.
10.

 **Pair Work**

Practice taking and placing a drink order replacing the underlined words.

> **A:** Can I take your order for a drink, first?
> **B:** Yes. I think I'll have <u>a cup of orange juice</u>.

60 CONNECTED 2

Conversation • What's New on the Menu Today?

1. Look at the picture and describe what is happening.

2. Listen to the conversation and fill in the blanks.

   Jennifer: Would you tell me what _____ are?

   Eric: Certainly. Our set menu begins with a _____ of soup or salad.

   Jennifer: What kind of soup is it?

   Eric: Today, it is broccoli cheese or potato bacon.

   Jennifer: And what is the _____?

   Eric: We have a beef steak or chicken breast served in wine sauce.

   All dishes are followed by _____.

   Jennifer: I'm on a diet. Can the dessert be changed to coffee?

   Eric: Of course. Would you like to try today's special?

   Jennifer: Yes, I would like the beef steak and salad with the coffee for dessert.

   Eric: Very good. Let me put in _____.

Pair Work

Practice taking and placing a food order replacing the underlined words.

> **A:** What would you like to have for your <u>main dish</u>?
>
> **B:** I would like to have <u>the steak and lobster</u>.

Unit 09 What's the Special Today?

Grammar Point • Modal Verbs 2

Polite Offers	Polite Responses
Can (Could) I + *verb*...? **Shall** I + *verb* ... for you? **Would you like** + *noun*? **Would you like me to** + *verb*...? **I'll** + *verb*... if you like.	Yes, please. I'd like to *verb*... If you wouldn't mind. / If you could. No, thanks. / No, thank you. Yes, please. That would be very kind of you. Yes, please. That would be lovely / great. Thank you. I'd love one.
Polite Requests / Asking for Permission	**Polite Responses**
Would you mind + *verb-ing*...? **Would you mind if I** + *verb*...?	No, not at all. / Sure. / All right. No, go ahead. / That's okay. / No, it's fine.

1. Complete the sentences with the correct words: *like*, *like to*, or *mind*.

1. Would you _____ another cup of coffee?
2. Would you _____ have a couple more of these appetizers?
3. Would you _____ if I take this plate, sir?
4. Would you _____ have an English menu?
5. Would you _____ waiting here for a minute?

2. Choose the correct answers to complete the sentence.

1. Would you like _____ to my house for dinner?
   a. come b. to come c. for to come d. coming

2. I _____ to work with animals in the future.
   a. shall b. would mind c. would like d. can

3. A: _____ I take your order? B: Yes, please.
   a. Can b. Might c. Would like d. Would

4. A: _____ you like to go out with me later? B: Sorry, but I can't.
   a. Would b. Could c. Shall d. Can

5. _____ buying two loaves of bread on your way home?
   a. Could you b. Will you c. Would you d. Would you mind

Pair Work Practice giving polite offers and responding to them replacing the underlined words.

A: Would you like <u>some more tea</u>?   B: <u>Yes, please. That would be very kind of you.</u>

Reading • The World's First Cafe in Venice

1. Think about the nicest cafe you've been to. What do you most like about it?

Café Florian

№ 34747/53
founded 1953

Café Florian opened on December 29th in 1720 and is one of the most well-known historical coffee shops in the world. Café Florian was reported to be the first place in Europe to serve coffee. It is located in San Marco Square, Italy. People can enjoy the view of the Basilica and Campanile. There are many lovely cafes around the sides of Piazza San Marco. The inside of Café Florian looks nice, and there are terraces with classical music playing on schedule outside. There is an additional charge if the music is playing when you order. The cafe has small rooms with marble topped tables and chairs. The waiters in white tuxedos with bow ties are elegant. The rooms are highly decorated with old paintings, mirrors, and red and gold wallpapers everywhere. They also have been decorated with the works of artists, sculptors, photographers, and cartoonists. Ricardo Selvatico was inspired while dining in the Senate Hall, and his suggestion made the Florian home into the International Exhibition of Contemporary Art, an ever-changing display of works of the artists of the time since 1893.

[Roading Skill: Cause and Effect] Go to Page 104.

2. Read the passage. Write *T* for true or *F* for false for each statement.

1. Café Florian is the cafe that first served coffee in Europe. _____
2. Inside the cafe, there is classical music playing on schedule. _____
3. There are many works of artists, sculptors, photographers, and cartoonists in the cafe. _____

Group Work

Discuss these questions in a group.
- What are the cafes like in your country?
- If you have your own cafe, how would you like to design the interior?

• Listen Up • **Would You Mind If I Order First?**

1. Getting Ready Listen and write the name of the person under the correct picture.

Daniel	Annie	Doug	Charles

_____ _____ _____ _____

2. Easy Listening Listen to the dialogue and answer the questions.

1. Why does the man say, "Excuse me."?
   a. He bumped into the woman.   b. The woman cut in line.

2. Why does the woman ask if she can order first?
   a. She is running late.   b. She needs to buy only one thing.

3. What does the woman want to do for the man?
   a. say thank you   b. pay for his order

3. Hard Rock Listen to the dialogue and answer the questions.

1. How many volunteers is the staff looking for?
   a. one   b. two

2. What is being offered to the man and woman for changing their flight?
   a. free flights   b. upgrades to first class

4. Pronunciation Blending of [w] and [ʊ]

Listen and practice. Notice the sound of [wʊ] in the following words.

	Correct	Incorrect
wolf	[wʊlf]	[ʊlf]
would / **wo**od	[wʊd]	[ʊd]
woman	[ˈwʊmən]	[ˈʊmən]

• Speaking Build-up • What Would You Like to Have?

1. Study the expressions to talk about what to order.

A: Hi, this is my first time here. <u>What do you recommend</u>?

B: Honestly, everything we make is the best.

A: Okay, but what is your personal favorite?

B: Well, if you like chicken, <u>our roast chicken is the best</u>.

A: What about something without meat?

B: Our vegetarian salad is the best in town.

A: Okay, I'll have the salad.

A
- What's good here?
- What's popular here?
- Are there any specials?

B
- I recommend our roast chicken.
- Would you like to try the roast chicken?

2. Look at the menu and choose what you'd like to have. Check (√) one from each of the starters, the main dishes, the desserts, and the beverages.

Menu		Price	
Starters	Chicken Salad	$3.50	
	Mushroom Soup	$3.00	
	French Fries	$3.50	
	Fried Clams	$4.00	
Main Dishes	Hamburger	$9.00	
	Steak	$15.00	
	Fried Chicken	$12.00	
	Steak and Lobster	$20.00	

Menu		Price	
Desserts	Cheesecake	$3.00	
	Ice Cream	$2.00	
	Brownie	$3.50	
Beverages	Soda	$1.50	
	Juice	$1.50	
	Milk	$1.00	
	Coffee	$1.00	

Pair Work Make dialogues about taking and placing an order using the menu above.

A: What would you like to have today?
B: I'd like to have <u>the fried clams and the steak</u>.

A: Would you like something to drink?
B: I will have <u>the juice</u>.

Culture Awareness — Tipping

In most restaurants in Europe and North and South America, the waiter usually makes very little money, often lower than the minimum wage. They live on their tips. A general rule is that you should leave 10% of your bill as a tip. For example, a $25 bill would earn a $2.50 tip. If you have good service, you can increase the amount. If you have really bad service, ask to see the manager. You might also want to see the manager if your service was really good.

[Writing: I Totally Recommend That You Go to That Restaurant!] Go to Page 105.

Review Units 07~09

• Conversation • Do You Always Fly First Class?

1. Listen to the conversation and fill in the blanks.

   Rachel: These seats are not that comfortable.
   Avion: They never are in _____.
   Rachel: I can't believe this is a _____.
   I know I'll get _____.
   Avion: Don't worry. You can _____ walk around a little during the flight.
   Rachel: Good to know. I'm getting hungry. Is there anything we can eat?
   Avion: We get a meal during the flight. Will you get the chicken or beef?
   Rachel: I'll try the chicken. What about you?
   Avion: I wonder if they have a _____.
   Rachel: I think they do. I forgot you don't like to eat meat.
   Avion: Well, _____ I try a little bit.
   Rachel: Look at the menu in the seat pocket.
   Avion: Oh good! They do have an option without meat!
   Rachel: At least this _____ has food on it.
   Avion: Yeah. Makes up for the uncomfortable _____.

2. Fill in the blank spaces with the proper frequency adverbs based on how often you do the following activities.

Always	Usually	Sometimes	Rarely	Never

Traveling on Airplane		Eating Out	
take non-stop flights		have a set menu	
fly economy class		order side dish(es)	
sit in an aisle seat		eat desserts	
get airsick		order today's special	
travel with a lot of luggage		leave a tip	

Pair Work Take turns asking and answering about your traveling and eating habits. Use the activities from the chart above to start your conversation.

A: Do you usually take non-stop flights or do you prefer the ones with layovers?
B: I normally take non-stop flights. I rarely take flights that have layovers.

• Reading • Airline Meals

Read the passage and choose the best answer to each question.

Everyone loves to talk about how great or awful airplane food can be – sometimes excellent, scrumptious, appetizing, incredible, but sometimes inedible, greasy, and disappointing. What is your most memorable airline meal?

Some airlines recruit for their "Flying Chef" program at Michelin-starred restaurants around the world. Their goal is to offer the service and standard that first class passengers would experience at a five-star restaurant.

Singapore Airlines offers passengers meals that are popular in each country along its main routes. Singapore Airlines is well-known for its wonderful and thoughtful service, and many passengers love the service and say they felt <u>pampered</u> even when flying economy.

Do you want to fly first class? If you are going to fly on Emirates airlines, don't count on getting a fancy seat. There's no time to sleep. Seven-course meals must be had. If you don't have much money, <u>don't fret</u>. The dinner for the economy class starts off with smoked tuna cut into thin slices. It is served with a vegetable salad. That is followed by lamb brochette which is accompanied with broccoli, roasted baby corn, and of course steamed white rice. To top it all off, they serve a sticky date pudding, crackers and cheese, chocolate, and brandy for those of legal drinking age. Why not explore the meals you can taste on international flights?

1. **What is the passage mainly about?**
   a. airline meals in each airline
   b. the cost of airline meals
   c. special airline meals
   d. the competition of airline meals

2. **What is the name of the program that some airlines recruited from Michelin-starred restaurants?**
   a. Flying Restaurant
   b. Flying Chef
   c. Flying Star Chef
   d. Flying Michelin

3. **What kind of food does Singapore Airlines offer to its passengers?**
   a. traditional meals from each country
   b. fresh meals from each country
   c. popular meals from each country
   d. unique meals from each country

4. **What is the meaning of the word "pampered" in the third paragraph?**
   a. treated with underserved food
   b. treated with inadequate service
   c. treated with too much excessive service
   d. treated with great service and fully satisfied

5. **Which phrase can replace "don't fret" in the fourth paragraph?**
   a. don't worry
   b. don't be confused
   c. don't leave
   d. don't be mad

UNIT 10　What's the Matter?

Vocabulary	Conversation	Grammar Point	Reading	Listen Up	Speaking Build-up
Health Problems	Get Well Soon!	Modal Verbs 3	Unhealthy Effects of Smartphones	Don't You Know That's Bad for You?	Are You Feeling Alright?

• Vocabulary • Health Problems

1. Study the expressions related to health problems.

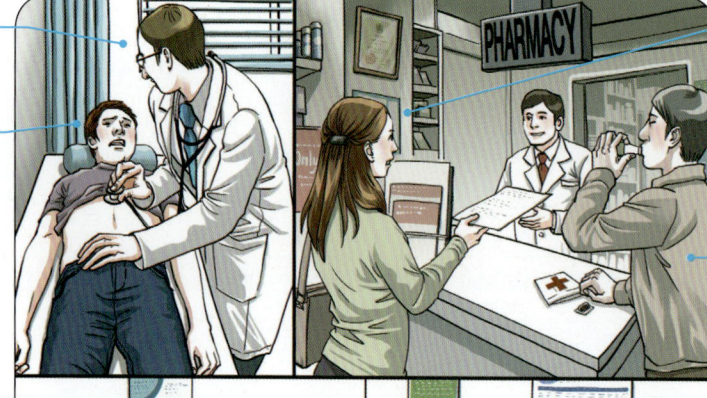

- **Doctor:** What's the matter?
- **Patient 1:** I have a stomachache.
- **Patient 2:** Can I get my prescription filled?
- **Patient 3:** I need to take this medicine twice a day.
- **Patient 4:** I feel nauseous.
- **Patient 5:** I have a broken leg.
- **Patient 6:** I have a headache.
- **Patient 7:** I have a fever.
- **Patient 8:** I'm very exhausted.
- **Patient 9:** I'm scared of injections!

2. Circle the correct word for each sentence.

1. When you feel pain in your head, you suffer from a (headache / stomachache).
2. When you feel like you might throw up, you feel (cold / nauseous).
3. When you have completely used up your energy, you are (scared / exhausted).

👥 Pair Work

Practice this dialogue replacing the underlined words.

> **A:** What is wrong with you? You don't look so good.
> **B:** I have a stomachache.

68　CONNECTED 2

• Conversation • **Get Well Soon!**

1. Look at the picture and describe what is happening.

2. Listen to the conversation and fill in the blanks.

Veronica: Are you feeling any better, Charles?
Charles: Not really, I still have a _____, and I'm still _____.
Veronica: Did you take the _____ the doctor gave you?
Charles: No, I forgot to get the _____ filled.
Veronica: You'll never get better if you don't take it.
Charles: You're right. Would you go to the pharmacy for me?
Veronica: Sure, I need your insurance card and the prescription.
Charles: Here they are. Thanks, Veronica.
Veronica: I'll be back in an hour. Rest. You look _____.
Charles: Okay. I will.

 Pair Work

Practice this dialogue replacing the underlined words.

A: You don't look well. What's wrong?
B: I'm just a little exhausted.

Grammar Point • Modal Verbs 3

Modals	Uses
must (more urgent) / **have to**	- to talk about something compulsory or very important - to talk about something that is true
should	- to say the right or correct thing to do - to give or ask for advice or suggestions - to say something is likely to happen
ought to	- to say the right or correct thing to do: something morally correct or polite

	Negative Forms	Questions
must	must not / musn't	Must you...?
have to	do not have to / don't have to	Do you have to...?
should	should not / shouldn't	Should you...?
ought to	ought not to / oughtn't to	Ought I (to)...?

1. Circle the correct modals.

1. Tim said he would come over right after work, so he (should / must) be here by 6:00.
2. I'd love to go on the cruise to Tahiti. But such a luxurious trip (must / should) cost a fortune.
3. I failed the math test, so I (have to / ought to) study hard from now on.
4. You (don't have to / ought not to) say such words to them. They're only children.

2. Choose the correct answers.

1. It's not obligatory to wear a tie. You _____ wear one.
   a. mustn't   b. have to   c. shouldn't   d. don't have to

2. A: Are you going to the party? B: I promised to go. So I _____ go.
   a. should   b. might   c. don't have to   d. mustn't

3. Slow down, or we're going to have an accident. You _____ drive so fast.
   a. shouldn't   b. ought to   c. don't have to   d. should

4. Where's the toilet? I _____ go.
   a. mustn't   b. should   c. have to   d. might

5. You _____ be kidding! That can't be true.
   a. should   b. may   c. have to   d. must

 Pair Work Practice this dialogue replacing the underlined words.

> A: What should I do? I have <u>a high fever</u>.   B: You must <u>go see a doctor</u>.

• Reading • Unhealthy Effects of Smartphones

1. Think about the negative effects of smartphones on your health.

Ariel felt uncomfortable with her fingers and she had sore muscles. She decided to see a doctor and check her health. When she met a doctor, the doctor asked several questions.

1. Do you have pain in your back or neck muscles?
2. Do your eyes get tired easily? Or do you have an unclear vision, dizziness, and dry eyes?
3. Do you always check to make sure you have your smartphone with you and continuously worry about losing it somewhere if you cannot see or use your smartphone?
4. Have you ever experienced phantom vibrations when your smartphone wasn't actually vibrating?

She answered "Yes" for questions 1, 2, and 4. The doctor said her pains are smartphone-related syndromes.

One in every five people in the world own a smartphone these days, and more than 60% of the population fears losing or being without smartphones. Almost 90% of students experienced phantom vibrations. Almost every heavy smartphone user has pains in their fingers, necks, elbows, and muscles. The ways to break the addiction and recover your health are only by checking your phone during chosen hours, keeping your phone in your bag, and shutting your vibration function off. Ariel had injections in her fingers and got physical therapy for her back and neck.

[**Reading Skill:** Summary] Go to Page 106.

2. Read the passage and answer the following questions.

1. Which is NOT one of the questions that the doctor asked?
   a. Do you have pain in your back or neck muscles?
   b. Do you have an unclear vision, dizziness, and dry eyes?
   c. Do you continuously worry about losing the smartphone when you see it?
   d. Have you ever experienced phantom vibrations when your smartphone wasn't actually vibrating?

2. Where do heavy smartphone users have pains?
   _____

3. What is "phantom vibration syndrome"?
   It's the feeling that your phone is vibrating when _____.

Group Work

Discuss these questions in a group.
- How much time do you spend on your smartphone per day?
- What negative effects have you experienced from using a smartphone?

• **Listen Up** • **Don't You Know That's Bad for You?**

1. Getting Ready Check (√) the activities that are good for your health.

eating junk food	eating vegetables	sleeping 8 hours a day	drinking water
drinking alcohol	taking a nap	taking vitamins	eating sweets

2. Easy Listening Listen to the dialogue and answer the questions.

1. What is the man eating?
   a. a hot dog   b. tacos

2. Why is the woman worried about what the man is eating?
   a. He's eating too much of it.   b. He's eating something bad for his health.

3. Why should the man eat more fruits and vegetables?
   a. They taste good.   b. They are good for him.

3. Hard Rock Listen to the dialogue and answer the questions.

1. What are the man and woman getting ready for?
   a. running   b. exercising

2. What does the woman have in her drink bottle?
   a. sports drink   b. water

4. Pronunciation Reduced Sound of *to*

Listen and practice. Notice the reduced sound of *to* in *have to* or *has to*.

[hæf tə]   I don't know if they have to go or not.
           You have to pay attention in class.

[hæs tə]   He has to win this match, or he is out of the game.
           She has to do her homework tonight.

• Speaking Build-up • Are You Feeling Alright?

1. Study the expressions to talk about physical conditions.

A: <u>Are you all right?</u> You don't look well.
B: <u>I'm feeling a little light-headed.</u>
A: You should sit down.
B: Thank you.
A: Are you any better?
B: A little bit. Could I have some water, please?
A: Sure, just a moment. And let me bring some aspirins, too.
B: Ah, thank you.

A
- Are you okay?
- Are you feeling okay?

B
- I have a headache.
- I feel a little dizzy.

2. Read the symptoms the people have and fill in the suggestions you would give to them.

	Latisha	Yuriko	Jeremiah
Symptoms	headache, throbbing pulse, sensitive to light and sound	fever, nausea, dizziness, and body aches	belly cramps, gas, pain, and constipation
Suggestions	• Go and sit in a cool dark room. • Put a cool wet cloth on your forehead. • Take some aspirins.		

Pair Work Take turns saying about health problems and giving advice. Use the expressions and suggestions in the chart above.

A: I have <u>a fever and a headache</u>.   B: Maybe you should get <u>enough rest and drink a lot of water</u>.

Culture Awareness — Sick Days

It is very common in Asia to see someone who is sick wearing a mask in public to keep others from getting sick. In most western countries, this is not done. If you are truly sick, stay home and rest. Your boss may get angry at you, but spreading the cold to your workplace could be a bigger mistake. Most companies allow a certain number of days for you to use when you are sick. If you are sick, go see a doctor and get well soon.

[Writing: How Do You Keep Yourself So Healthy?] Go to Page 107.

UNIT 11

Vocabulary	Conversation	Grammar Point	Reading	Listen Up	Speaking Build-up
Telecommunications	Would You Help Me with This?	Causative Verbs	New Film Casting	How Do You Communicate?	Please, Check Your Messages

Did You Get My Text Message?

• Vocabulary • Telecommunications

1. Choose the correct word for each number and write the letter.

a. reply	b. text message	c. email address	d. attachment
e. blind carbon copy	f. carbon copy	g. emoticon	h. delete

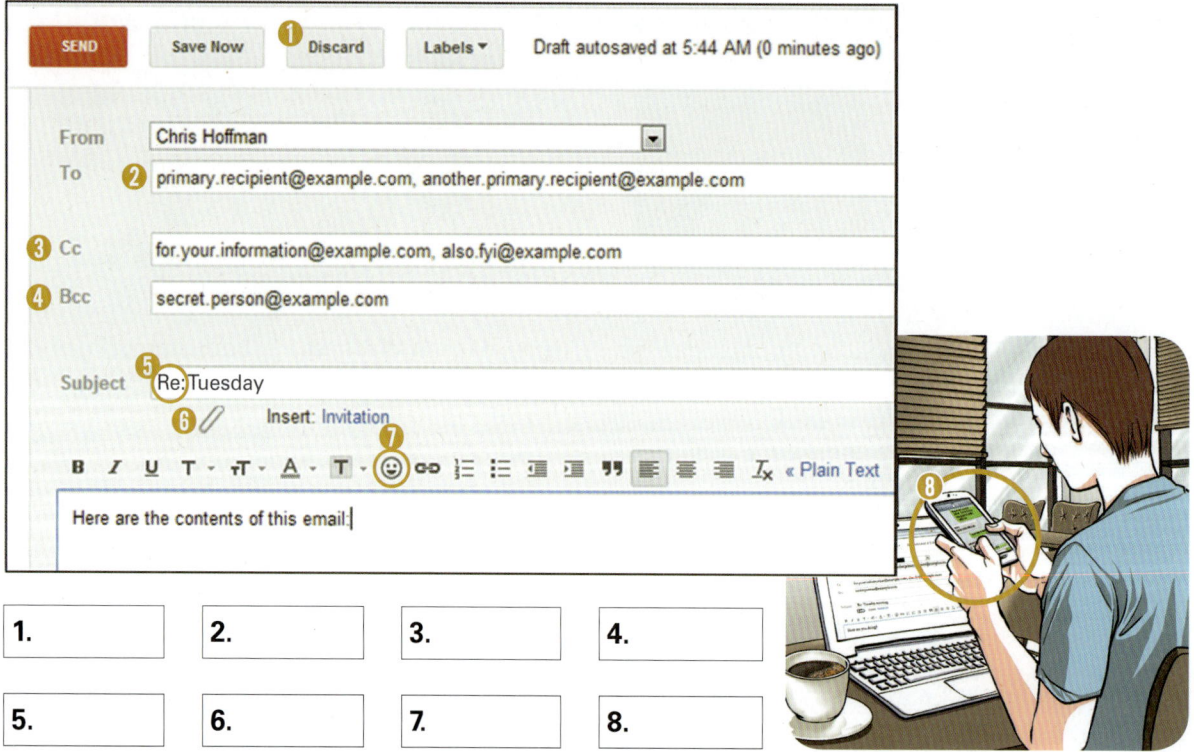

1. ____ 2. ____ 3. ____ 4. ____

5. ____ 6. ____ 7. ____ 8. ____

 **Pair Work**

Practice this dialogue replacing the underlined words.

A: How can I contact <u>you</u>?

B: You can contact <u>me</u> by <u>phone</u>.

• **Conversation** • **Would You Help Me with This?**

1. Look at the picture and describe what is happening.

2. Listen to the conversation and fill in the blanks.

Joy: Can you help me with this?

Sam: Sure, what's up?

Joy: I need to send _____ to make an appointment on behalf of my boss by email. Can you look at it first?

Sam: Of course. Send it to me.

Joy: I already did. Check your _____.

Sam: I don't see it. Let me check my _____ folder… Got it.

Joy: So, what do you think?

Sam: It's not bad. But let me highlight the parts you should _____. And you shouldn't use emoticons. They look unprofessional.

Joy: Thanks, I'll edit and send it. And I'll CC you on the message.

Sam: Make it _____. I don't want the boss to know I'm helping you.

Joy: Will do. Thanks again.

Pair Work Practice this dialogue replacing the underlined words.

> **A:** I sent you <u>an email</u> yesterday. Did you get it?
> **B:** Yes, I received it. / No, I haven't checked it yet.

• Grammar Point • Causative Verbs

	Structure	Uses	Examples
let	<u>let</u> + object + verb	to allow or give permission	Barry *let* me *use* his car.
make	<u>make</u> + object + verb / p.p	to force an action	He *made* me *clean* the room.
have	<u>have</u> + object + verb / p.p	to give responsibility to do something	I *had* her *feed* the cat. He will *have* his phone *repaired*.
get	<u>get</u> + object + to verb / p.p	to convince a result	I *got* him *to stop* smoking. I *get* my teeth *cleaned* every year.
help	<u>help</u> + object + verb / to verb	to give support	He *helped* me *carry* the boxes.

1. Complete the sentences with the correct causative verbs: *let, make, have, get,* or *help.*

1. **A:** Did your wife _____ you clean the house?   **B:** Of course. She dusted the rugs.
2. She _____ him to stop crying by giving him a sweet.
3. Please _____ the delivery placed in front of the house.
4. Tim's parents _____ him apologize for breaking the window.
5. They really wanted to go hiking, but the ranger wouldn't _____ them do so.

2. Choose the correct words to replace the underlined words.

1. My sister <u>persuaded</u> me to take out the garbage.
   a. made b. let c. got d. had

2. Who <u>forced you to do</u> that?
   a. made you do b. made you to do c. make you do d. made you doing

3. The boss <u>asked us to do</u> a presentation.
   a. had us to do b. got us to do c. had us do d. got us do

4. What didn't your parents <u>allow you to do</u> when you were a kid?
   a. get you do b. let you do c. let you to do d. make you to do

5. I <u>gave him a hand to clean</u> the kitchen.
   a. had him clean b. made him clean c. had him to clean d. helped him clean

 Pair Work Practice using causative verbs replacing the underlined words.

A: Would you <u>have him clean the room</u>?   **B:** I will <u>have him do the laundry</u>, too.

Reading — New Film Casting

 Online Practice

UNIT 11

1. Think about the most touching movie you've ever seen. Who starred in the movie?

From: James Silverman
To: Brad Denvon, Bradley Addington
Cc: Leonardo Hull   **Bcc:** Scarlett Michael, Emma Robertson

Dear Brad and Bradley,

    What are you up to these days? It seems like you are busy with so many things to promote your movies. I have been busy with my new movie preparation. And I would like to offer two of you roles in my new film as the two main characters. Some actors are already cast. Please, read the script I sent you and let me know if you are interested. I am 100 percent certain you are the only people who can manage the roles in this production. Leo accepted a cameo part, so I CC'd him. Hans Reeves will be in charge of music. He has worked on the Lion King, the Dark Knight, Inception, and many others as you know. Eric Roth, the screenwriter for the Curious Case of Benjamin Button and Forrest Gump and Baz Luhrmann of the Great Gatsby will help me complete the script. We also have great staff ready to help you!

I look forward to meeting you for this production soon.

Sincerely,

James Silverman

[Reading Skill: Identifying Pronoun References**]** Go to Page 108.

2. Read the email and answer the following questions.

1. Who is sending this email? _____
2. Who is going to get this email? _____
3. Who is going to read this email without letting others know?
   _____

 **Group Work**

Discuss these questions in a group.

- What do you use emails for?
- What are the advantages and disadvantages of using emails?

Unit 11 Did You Get My Text Message?

Listen Up • How Do You Communicate?

1. Getting Ready Number the means of communication from the fastest to the slowest.

	postal mail		telephone call		mobile phone call		fax
	instant messenger		email		delivery service		text message

2. Easy Listening Listen to the dialogue and answer the questions.

1. Why is the man angry with the woman?
   a. She made a mistake.   b. She was late for work.

2. Why did the man change his phone number?
   a. Maryann kept calling him.   b. He lost his phone.

3. What does the woman say she won't do?
   a. give his number to others   b. talk about his friends

3. Hard Rock Listen to the dialogue and answer the questions.

1. Who is the man talking to on the phone?
   a. a sales person   b. a representative of the customer suppor

2. Why is the man calling the customer support team?
   a. He didn't get his order.   b. He got the wrong package.

4. Pronunciation Distinguishing between *L* and *R* Sounds
Listen and practice. Notice the different [l] and [r] sounds in the words.

leaf	reef	real
full	care	carefully
fail	fair	fairly

78 CONNECTED 2

Speaking Build-up • Please, Check Your Messages

1. Study the expressions to see whether text messages have been checked.

A: Did you get the message I sent you yesterday?
B: I'm sorry, I didn't. I was in church yesterday.
A: I needed to get your help about a problem.
B: Is there any way I can help now?
A: No, but please check your messages.
B: I usually do, but in the church I turn my phone off.
A: I understand. You don't actually have to turn it off, you know. You can put it on silent mode.
B: Oh, OK. I will try that next time.

A
- Could you check your messages?
- Please respond to my message.
- Respond ASAP!

2. Look at the list of Internet acronyms. Try to write what each of the acronyms stands for. Try not to use the Internet to look them up.

LOL	1. Laughing Out Loud 2. Lots of Love	TMI/WTMI		BTW	
ASL		TTYL		OMG	
FYI		ROFL		BRB	
TY/THX		ASAP/AQAP		YOLO	

Pair Work Write short messages using the acronyms above. Take turn reading the messages out loud and respond to them.

A: TTYL   B: OK. LOL.

Culture Awareness — Communication Etiquette

The 21st century has found us super connected to the world. Almost everyone has a cell phone, and communication is nearly instantaneous. Take some time and disconnect yourself from your phone for a little while every day. Mealtimes are a great time to turn off the ringer and enjoy the company. Also, be sure to turn your cell phone to silent mode in special locations: religious centers, movie theaters, hospitals, funeral homes, etc.

[Writing: Do You Have Time to Meet on Monday?] Go to Page 109.

UNIT 12

Vocabulary College Campus | **Conversation** How Long Does It Take to Get There? | **Grammar Point** Questions With *How* | **Reading** Campus Tour | **Listen Up** When Will It Be Ready? | **Speaking Build-up** How Can I Go to the Chemistry Department?

I'm Looking for the Student Union

• Vocabulary • College Campus

 Online Practice

1. Choose the correct word for each picture and write the letter.

a. auditorium
b. library
c. laboratory
d. Student Union
e. dormitory
f. College of Engineering
g. campus
h. theater
i. cafeteria

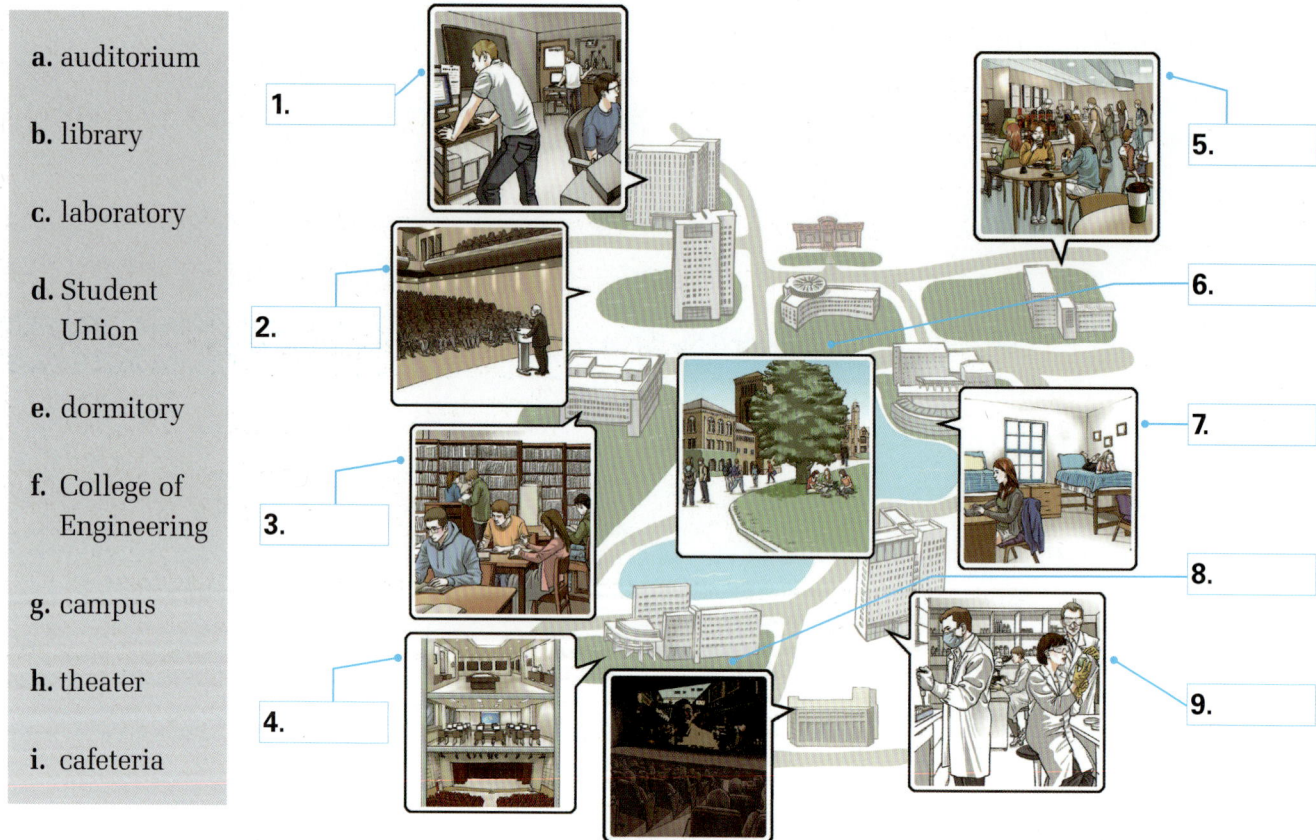

2. Fill in the blanks with the correct words from the box above.

1. The orchestra is entering the _____ to perform before an audience.
2. _____ offers students various facilities such as meeting spaces and dining areas.
3. Lisa is living in the college _____ with a roommate.

👥 Pair Work

Ask and answer about locations of buildings in a college campus.

A: Where is <u>the library</u>?   B: It is <u>next to the Student Union building</u>.

80 CONNECTED 2

• Conversation • **How Long Does It Take to Get There?**  UNIT 12

1. Look at the picture and describe what is happening.

2. Listen to the conversation and fill in the blanks.

Daniel: Excuse me. Could you tell me how to get to the _____?

Holli: Sure. Go up this road until you see the _____ building.

Daniel: Where do I go from there?

Holli: The engineering building is right next to it.

Daniel: How much time will it take?

Holli: It's going to take you about 10 minutes.

Daniel: Can you show me where we are on the _____?

Holli: Sure, we are here and this is the _____.

Daniel: I see where I am. Thanks.

Pair Work

Ask and answer about how long it takes to get to a place in a college campus.

A: How long will it take me to get to the administration building?

B: It's about a ten-minute walk.

Unit 12 I'm Looking for the Student Union

• Grammar Point • Questions with *How*

Questions	Answers
How much does this phone cost?	It costs **100 dollars**.
How many people are there in this country?	There are about **51 million people**.
How often do you go on a trip?	I go on a trip **twice a year**.
How long will it take to get there?	It will take **three hours** by car.
How far is the bus station?	It is **50 meters** from here.
How high is the Eiffel Tower?	It is **324 meters** high.

1. Complete the sentences with the correct words.

1. How _____ coffee do you drink a day?
2. How _____ students are there in this class?
3. **A:** How _____ do you visit Japan?   **B:** Three times a year.
4. **A:** How _____ do you swim on Sundays?   **B:** Two hours.
5. **A:** How _____ are you at cooking?   **B:** Not bad.

2. Choose the correct answers.

1. _____ work do you have to do today?
   a. How long   b. How many   c. How much   d. How far

2. How _____ is the Mississippi River?
   a. many   b. much   c. tall   d. long

3. **A:** How _____ is the exam?   **B:** It's not easy!
   a. difficult   b. big   c. long   d. far

4. **A:** How old are you?   **B:** _____.
   a. It was long ago.   b. It's been 20 years.
   c. In 1987.   d. I'm twenty-three.

5. **A:** How much is the cruise?   **B:** _____.
   a. It's 1,450 Euros.   b. It's three times a month.
   c. It's 670 kilometers.   d. It's 10 days.

Pair Work

Practice asking and answering questions using the question word *how*.

A: How many hours a day do you study?   **B:** I usually study five to six hours a day.

• Reading • Campus Tour

1. What does your college campus look like? Are you familiar with the way around the campus?

If you are visiting our campus for the first time, spend an hour and a half with a cheerful student guide exploring the highlights of this beautiful campus for free. It would be a great introduction for first-time visitors and tourists. The Campus Walking Tour departs from the Visitor Center. The Visitor Center will be closed on weekends. The tour, however, will still be offered each day at 11:00 a.m. and 3:00 p.m. This tour covers the central campus. First, the Main Quad is the historic and academic center of campus and includes the school of Humanities & Sciences. You can also visit Memorial Church. It is at the center of campus and the University's architectural crown jewel. The Science and Engineering Quad is a popular stop for visitors with many modern and stylish buildings. The Cantor Arts Center has its entire Rodin collection, 200 works in all, for public viewing. The Cantor's collection of Rodin bronzes is among the largest in the world. The Rodin Sculpture Garden is open 24 hours, with lighting for nighttime viewing. White Plaza is a student activities area. There are bookstores, student stores, the Old Union, and the Memorial Union. At the bookstore, you can buy T-shirts or pens for souvenirs.

[Reading Skill: Finding Supporting Details] Go to Page 110.

2. Read the passage. Write *T* for true or *F* for false for each statement.

1. The Campus Walking Tour would be a great introduction for first-time visitors and tourists. _____
2. The Visitor Center is open on weekends. _____
3. There are 200 works by Rodin in the Cantor Arts Center. _____

Group Work

Discuss this question in a group.

- If you were to guide a campus tour of your college, which place would you be most proud to introduce? And why?

• Listen Up • When Will It Be Ready?

1. **Getting Ready** Read the following questions first. Then listen to the responses and write the letter of the correct response to each question.

Questions	Responses
1. May I help you?	
2. What time can I pick that up?	
3. How much money would you like to spend?	
4. What else would you like on the cake?	

2. **Easy Listening** Listen to the dialogue and answer the questions.

   1. For what does the man need a cake?
      - a. a birthday
      - b. wedding anniversary

   2. What is going to be put on the cake?
      - a. fruits
      - b. flowers

   3. What time will the man pick up his order?
      - a. at 4:30
      - b. at 5

3. **Hard Rock** Listen to the dialogue and answer the questions.

   1. How much money does the woman have?
      - a. $25
      - b. $30

   2. What is the woman asking the man for?
      - a. different colors of the item
      - b. different sizes of the item

4. **Pronunciation** Reduced *-ing* Sound

   Listen and practice. Notice the reduced sound of *-ing* [ɪŋ] in the sentences.

I am ask**ing** for information.	They are hav**ing** lunch.
She is talk**ing** to a friend.	We will be wait**ing** downstairs for you.

84 CONNECTED 2

Speaking Build-up • How Can I Go to the Chemistry Department?

UNIT 12

1. Study the expressions to talk about the way around a college campus.

A: You look lost. What are you looking for?
B: I can't seem to find the chemistry department.
A: You are on the wrong side of campus for that.
B: Really? But isn't this the science building?
A: This is the natural science building. The chemistry department is located with engineering.
B: How long will it take to get there from here?
A: It's about a 15-minute walk, or five minutes if you catch the shuttle bus.
B: Thank you. I have to hurry. I'm late.

B
- How can I find the chemistry building?
- I'm looking for the chemistry department.

A
- I'm sorry, but it's on the other side of campus.
- I'm afraid it's located on the other side.

2. Imagine you are in the middle of a campus. Fill in the chart with the locations of two of the buildings and how long it takes to get there. Use *next to, near, between, on the left/right*, etc.

Building	Student Union		
Location	next to the library near the auditorium		
Time	a 15-minute walk		

Pair Work Ask and answer about where a building in a campus is located using the chart above.

A: Excuse me, I'm looking for the Student Union building, but I can't seem to find it.
B: The building is located next to the library near the auditorium.
A: Do you know how long it takes to get there?
B: It's about a 15-minute walk from here.

Culture Awareness — It's 10 Minutes away

In many places around the world, when you ask how far it is to a place, people will tell you how long it takes to get there. They are answering your question, but not answering it at the same time. This is an implied question. The literal answer might be "It's 500 meters that way." But many people will say "It's about 10 minutes that way." They are answering the unanswered question of how long it will take to get there. Although it is poor grammar, it is common in speech.

[Writing: Are You Looking for a Roommate?] Go to Page 111.

Review Units 10~12

• Conversation • You Should Be More Careful Next Time

1. Listen to the conversation and fill in the blanks.

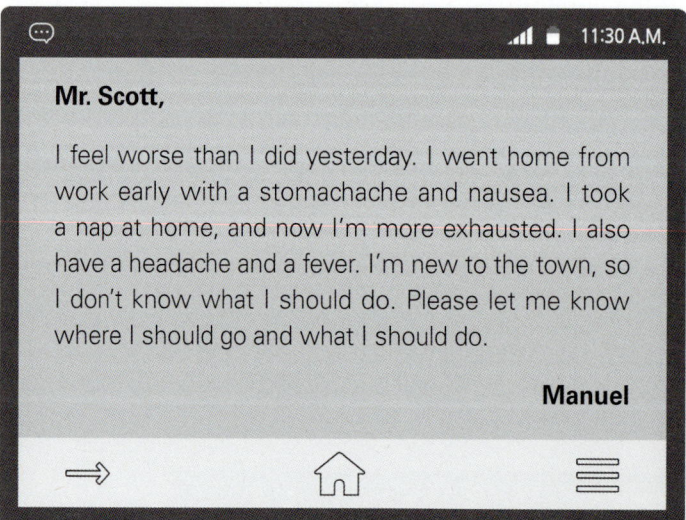

Cindy: Are you okay, Daniel?
Daniel: Not really, my leg _____.
Cindy: Why were you in such a hurry? You should be careful not to _____ again.
Daniel: I know, but I have an appointment in the _____ at four o'clock.
Cindy: Is that why you were walking so fast?
Daniel: Yeah, it's in a few minutes, and this is only the _____.
Cindy: Well, you should slow down now and rest your leg a little.
Daniel: Alright, I should _____ my friends know that I'll be late.
Cindy: Send a _____ immediately. Then let's go see a doctor.
Daniel: OK, thanks for the help.

2. Read the following text message. What suggestions would you make to the person?

> Mr. Scott,
>
> I feel worse than I did yesterday. I went home from work early with a stomachache and nausea. I took a nap at home, and now I'm more exhausted. I also have a headache and a fever. I'm new to the town, so I don't know what I should do. Please let me know where I should go and what I should do.
>
> Manuel

Pair Work Talk about the suggestions you would give to Manuel. Use the following questions to keep the conversation going.

- Where do you think he should go?
- What should he do?
- How can he get the help he needs?

86 CONNECTED 2

Reading • Campus Life and Healthcare

Read the passage and choose the best answers.

The University of Oxford is one of the world's most beautiful campuses. This 11th century campus has its maze of arcades, archways, and pathways – an architectural wonderland. Oxford's stone walls date as far back as the 11th century, and the school is considered a model for all college campuses. The famous Radcliffe Camera was built in 1737 as a science building, and now it is a silent reading room for students. It is the most desirable university building in the world. You can get the most out of life as a student in Oxford. You can find out about accommodation, gain work experience, join societies, have healthcare services, travel, and provide feedback.

The University of Oxford understands how important it is for students and their families to know they have access to high quality healthcare away from home. The Student Health Service (SHS) healthcare providers work hard to provide that care. You will enjoy access to the full service primary care clinic once you are enrolled as a student at Oxford University. The clinic staff will take the time to get to know you and address your personal medical needs and care. The nationally certified nurses and doctors will guide and assist you through any and all health issues that you may encounter while you are a student. Some of the most common ailments that occur are colds and sore throats. The staff can help you with vaccinations, physical lab work, asthma flare-ups, and even refilling your medication. The SHS providers will make sure you have excellent total care in a confidential setting.

1. **What is the passage mainly about?**
   a. the campus and the healthcare system in the University of Oxford
   b. introduction to Oxford University buildings
   c. the Student Health Service in England
   d. introduction to a full-service medical clinic

2. **When was this campus built?**
   a. in the 10th century
   b. in the 11th century
   c. in the 12th century
   d. in the 13th century

3. **What is the use of the Radcliffe Camera building now?**
   a. a science building
   b. a hospital
   c. a silent reading room for students
   d. a chapel

4. **Who is the Oxford Student Health Service for?**
   a. enrolled students
   b. professors
   c. their faculty's families
   d. students and their families

5. **What is NOT provided by the Oxford Student Health Service?**
   a. care for colds or sore throats
   b. vaccinations
   c. treatment for a flare-up of asthma
   d. service for building up a healthy body

Unit 01

• Reading Skill • Using Context Clues

Context clues are the hints in a sentence or a passage. They can help you infer a word you don't know and understand the meaning of the word. The clue may appear in the same sentence.

Build up the Skill

Read the paragraphs and answer the questions.

> When Henry's boss went on maternity leave, Henry became the interim department head. He handled employee payroll for three months while his boss was away.

1. What does "interim" most likely mean?

    a. temporary   b. new   c. longtime   d. old

> Joan wanted to turn left on King Street. However, the fog was very thick, making it difficult to see. So instead, she inadvertently turned on to Sunny Street.

2. What does "inadvertently" most likely mean?

    a. carefully   b. intentionally   c. unintentionally   d. consciously

> Ellen learns more from her experiences than what she studies in school. Her marks on exams attest to many hours of her hard work.

3. What does "attest" most likely mean?

    a. give proof of   b. honor   c. argue   d. result

> Daniel cleaned his desk and computer. He put all of his papers into neat and well-ordered piles. He then stood up and pushed his chair under his desk. This was his habit at the end of each workday. At his home, he was equally meticulous about keeping things neat and clean.

4. What does "meticulous" most likely mean?

    a. general   b. careful   c. casual   d. overall

> Searching for students' lockers without permission is considered to be an <u>infringement</u> of students' rights.

5. What does "infringement" most likely mean?

   a. help	b. sample	c. example	d. violation

• Writing • What Did You Do Next?

1. Pre-writing Answer the following questions to prepare to write.

- What did you do last Sunday?
- Where did you go?
- Who did you meet?
- What did you talk about?
- Did anything special happen?
- What did you do after that?

2. Writing the First Draft Write about what you did last Sunday. Use the answers from the Pre-writing activity to organize your writing. Focus on the sequence of the events.

> **Example** Last Sunday was a busy day for me. I woke up early and went to church. The service was long but interesting. After that, I had lunch at a local restaurant. Then I met my best friend in the Internet cafe, and we played computer games for a few hours. I went home in the evening and started doing my homework. After I had finished my homework, I took a shower and went to bed.

3. Peer Review Exchange your writing with a partner. Then read your partner's writing and look for mistakes or errors. Make corrections on them and return the writing to your partner.

4. Rewriting Look at the corrections that your partner made and revise your writing based on the corrections. Try to rewrite the parts you'd like to change in order to improve your writing.

Unit 02

• Reading Skill • Making Inferences

Inferences are ideas that have been suggested by the details or facts in a passage.

Making inferences requires the readers to fill in blanks left out by the author. Authors may leave out the information because they think you already know it, it may be unimportant to the author, or it may be a way to have you look for the answer or information for yourself.

Build up the Skill

Read the paragraphs and answer the questions.

> Tiffany went to the closet and grabbed her umbrella in the morning. But soon she almost wished that she hadn't listened to the radio. She felt silly carrying it to the bus stop on such a sunny morning.

1. **Which of the following probably happened?**
    a. Tiffany realized that she had an unnatural fear of taking a radio apart.
    b. Tiffany had promised herself to do something silly that morning.
    c. Tiffany had heard a weather forecast that predicted rain.
    d. Tiffany planned to trade her umbrella for a bus ride.

> "Larry, first of all, I have to tell you that it has been very interesting working with you. As your boss, you have surprised me quite often." Miss Valdez said. "However, your performance style and what the company expects don't match up very well. I must, therefore, ask you to resign your position. This will be effective as of today."

2. **What was Miss Valdez telling Larry?**
    a. That she would feel really bad if he decided to quit.
    b. That he was fired.
    c. That he was getting a raise.
    d. That she really enjoyed having him in the office.

> Jessica and Bill were selecting players for their teams for an upcoming game. They were nearly finished. There was only one person left, Kurt. It was Jessica's turn, and she reluctantly said, "Kurt."

3. **What can be inferred from the paragraph?**
   a. Kurt is not a very good player.
   b. Jessica was pleased to have Kurt on her team.
   c. Kurt was the best player on both teams.
   d. Jessica was considerate of Kurt's feelings.

• Writing • Let the Festivities Begin!

1. **Pre-writing** Answer the following questions to prepare to write.

   - What is the most important holiday in your country?
   - How do people celebrate this holiday?
   - Are there any special clothes or ornaments for the holiday?
   - Is this holiday celebrated outside of your country, too?

2. **Writing the First Draft** Write about one of the most important holidays in your country. Use the answers from the Pre-writing activity to organize your writing.

   > **Example** In Mexico, we celebrate "El Dia de los Muertos" of the Day of the Dead. It begins on October 31st and ends on November 2nd. It is a time to honor those that have passed away. We usually use marigolds, a type of flower to decorate the tombs. Toys are often brought to the tombs of children who have died, while tequila or other alcohol is brought for adults.

3. **Peer Review** Exchange your writing with a partner. Then read your partner's writing and look for mistakes or errors. Make corrections on them and return the writing to your partner.

4. **Rewriting** Look at the corrections that your partner made and revise your writing based on the corrections. Try to rewrite the parts you'd like to change in order to improve your writing.

Unit 03

• Reading Skill • Identifying the Topic and Main Idea

Topic is the general subject of a written passage.
Main idea shows the topic and the point of a passage.
Identifying the topic can help you find the author's **main idea**.
A paragraph usually includes: *topic, main idea (or topic sentence), and supporting details.*

Build up the Skill

Read the paragraphs and answer the questions.

> There were many reasons why my family enjoys traveling. Firstly, the journey gives us a new experience and adventure. Secondly, we can spend all our time together during the trip. And thirdly it gives us a chance to understand each other better.

1. What is the main idea of the paragraph?

    a. There were many reasons why my family enjoys traveling.
    b. The journey gives us new experience and adventure.
    c. We can spend all our time together during the trip.
    d. We can understand each other better.

> University students can make their own career decision by internships. They can have work experience and transportable skills and experience a prospective career path. They can also make money. Best of all is to have a network with specialists in the field and references for future job opportunities.

2. What is the main idea of the paragraph?

    a. University students can have a network with specialists in the field and references for future job opportunities.
    b. University students can make their own career decision by internships.
    c. University students can have work experience and transportable skills.
    d. University students can earn money.

> Air pollution in Korea has increased more and more in recent years. The fine dust in the air of Seoul, for example, can block the sunshine and cause people to have more respiratory distress. Especially, the dust from China in spring and fall is getting serious. The Korean government and companies try to assist China to decrease the yellow Asian dust.

3. What is the main idea of the paragraph?

   a. The fine dust blocks the sunshine and makes people have more respiratory diseases.

   b. The Korean government and companies try to assist China to decrease the yellow Asian dust.

   c. Air pollution in Korea has increased more and more in recent years.

   d. Especially, the dust from China in spring and fall is getting serious.

• Writing • That Was the Best / Worst Trip Ever!

1. Pre-writing Answer the following questions to prepare to write.

> - What is the best / worst trip you've ever taken?
> - Where did you go?
> - Who did you go with?
> - Why was it the best / worst?
> - Would you like to travel back to the place again?

2. Writing the First Draft Write about the best or worst trip you've taken. Use the answers from the Pre-writing activity to organize your writing.

> **Example** A few years ago, I took a trip to Taiwan. It turned out to be the best and the worst trip I have ever taken. It was the best because the scenery and sights were amazing. Especially, Taroko Gorge and Taipei 101 were absolutely amazing. But I wish I had traveled with people I knew. I went on a tour with strangers, and it didn't turn out as well as I hoped. I want to travel back to Taiwan with my friends again, if I can.

3. Peer Review Exchange your writing with a partner. Then read your partner's writing and look for mistakes or errors. Make corrections on them and return the writing to your partner.

4. Rewriting Look at the corrections that your partner made and revise your writing based on the corrections. Try to rewrite the parts you'd like to change in order to improve your writing.

Unit 04

• Reading Skill • Distinguishing Facts from Opinions

A fact states something that:

- **happens**
  A lunar eclipse happens when the Moon passes through the shadow of the Earth.
- **has happened or is certain to be true**
  Thomas Jefferson wrote the Declaration of Independence.
- **is real or exists**
  The sun is a star.

An opinion states something:

- **believed to have occurred**
  We had a pop quiz today in math class because the teacher got angry.
- **believed to exist**
  The subway station is near to my house, so I can't miss the subway.
- **believed to be true**
  Grandma and Grandpa love me the most.

Build up the Skill

Read each statement and identify whether it is a fact, an opinion or both.
(* Facts and opinions are NOT always easily identifiable or separable.)

1. The Earth is round. _____
2. Summer follows spring. _____
3. In 2010, the 19th World Cup was held in South Africa. _____
4. The British winter of 2009/2010 was the coldest in 30 years. _____
5. I think that rock music is awful. _____
6. The legal drinking age should be lowered from 18 to 16. _____
7. New York is the best city in the world. _____
8. Today seems hotter than yesterday. _____
9. You are studying at a university. _____
10. You are studying at a good university. _____
11. It is one of the best in Japan. _____
12. If we used mass transportation more, there would be fewer cars on the road. That would reduce air pollution and noise from traffic. _____

• Writing • What Are Your Holiday Plans?

1. Pre-writing Answer the following questions to prepare to write.

> Imagine you're going away for an upcoming holiday.
> - Where are you going?
> - What are you planning to do?
> - Who are you traveling with?
> - How are you going to get there?

2. Writing the First Draft Write about your plans for an upcoming holiday. Use the answers from the Pre-writing activity to organize your writing.

> **Example** This Thanksgiving, I am going to travel back home to be with my family. I live far away, so it is not often that I can visit them. I will take a flight for most of the way. I will also have to take a bus because my family lives far from the airport. I am going to stay there for five days and then come back to my place.

3. Peer Review Exchange your writing with a partner. Then read your partner's writing and look for mistakes or errors. Make corrections on them and return the writing to your partner.

4. Rewriting Look at the corrections that your partner made and revise your writing based on the corrections. Try to rewrite the parts you'd like to change in order to improve your writing.

Unit 05

• Reading Skill • Identifying the Topic and Main Idea

Topic is the general subject of a piece of writing.
Main idea is usually stated in a sentence and includes the main topic and point.

Build up the Skill

Write the topic and the main idea of each paragraph.

> Water is an amazing resource. Everyone in the world depends upon it. Every creature needs water to survive. Without water, we cannot live. Water makes our world sustainable.

1. The topic is _____.

2. The main idea is that _____.

> Colonial Williamsburg, Virginia is a wonderful place to visit. When you visit Williamsburg you can see what it was like to live in the 18th century. The town is staffed by people and guides in costume who will help you explore what colonial America was like. They will take you to various taverns, shops, and houses. Some of the taverns offer you colonial food. Visiting Williamsburg will let you feel like you have stepped into a time machine and visit the United States while it was still a part of Great Britain.

3. The topic is _____.

4. The main idea is that _____.

> In the Atlantic Ocean, there is a very special island called Assateague Island. It is home to famous wild horses, foxes, and seagulls. The small island is covered with long sandy beaches. It is an amazing place to visit and view its animals and beaches.

7. The topic is _____.

8. The main idea is that _____.

• Writing • That Was the Strangest Food

1. Pre-writing Answer the following questions to prepare to write.

- Are you an adventurous eater?
- What is the weirdest food you have ever eaten?
- Have you ever had food that is still alive or just recently killed?
- Where did you have it?
- What was it like?

2. Writing the First Draft Write about the weirdest food or drink that you have had. Use the answers from the Pre-writing activity to organize your writing.

> **Example** In Taipei, Taiwan there is a place called snake alley. There people can get alcohol served with various fluids from a snake; blood, bile, and venom. My friends and I also ate snake meat. All of it was pretty good, but I would only recommend it for those who like a little adventure.

3. Peer Review Exchange your writing with a partner. Then read your partner's writing and look for mistakes or errors. Make corrections on them and return the writing to your partner.

4. Rewriting Look at the corrections that your partner made and revise your writing based on the corrections. Try to rewrite the parts you'd like to change in order to improve your writing.

Unit 06

• Reading Skill • Finding Supporting Details

> **A paragraph** contains facts, statements, examples, and specifics which guide us to a full understanding of the main idea. They clarify, illuminate, explain, describe, expand, and illustrate the main idea and **supporting details**.
>
> **Determining Supporting Details:**
> 1. Find which details help to move the story line forward.
> 2. Find what ideas help clarify and understand the main idea.
> 3. Answer the questions raised by the main idea (who, what, where, when, why, and how).

Build up the Skill

Choose the correct type of supporting details and write the letter.

> **a.** comparisons in which one is shown to be like the other
> **b.** contrasts in which one is shown to differ from the other
> **c.** statistics
> **d.** graphs
> **e.** quotations from authorities
> **f.** vivid descriptions

1. _____ Both skilled and unskilled college students are alike in their desire for a diploma or a degree.

2. _____ "At the beginning of the semester, I always tell my students that they don't have to attend my classes. But, I know they won't pass my course if they DON'T attend." Admitted Professor Smith.

3. _____ What you see in Figure 3-1 is one type of graph.

4. _____ Nearly 75 percent of students who received C or worse, do not attend class on a regular basis.

5. _____ Unskilled students are often different from skilled students because they don't use helpful methods to read a textbook.

6. _____ After taking the exam quickly from the professor's hand, and glancing at the marked grade, the student gave a sigh of relief and then began to smile.

• Writing • Wow, That Hurts!

1. Pre-writing Answer the following questions to prepare to write.

- Were you ever hurt in an accident?
- Have you ever been hit by a car or other moving vehicles?
- Have you ever received a speeding ticket?
- Have you ever had a close call or near miss?

If you have never experienced any of the above, recall someone else's experiences that you know.

2. Writing the First Draft Write about an accident or an incident that has happened to you or someone you know. Use the answers from the Pre-writing activity to organize your writing. Focus on the sequence of the events.

> **Example** Last year, I was walking to the bus stop, and a car bumped me. It was turning, and its mirror hit my left arm. Fortunately, the car wasn't going very fast. It bruised my arm a little, but nothing was broken. The driver stopped, looked at me, and then sped away.

3. Peer Review Exchange your writing with a partner. Then read your partner's writing and look for mistakes or errors. Make corrections on them and return the writing to your partner.

4. Rewriting Look at the corrections that your partner made and revise your writing based on the corrections. Try to rewrite the parts you'd like to change in order to improve your writing.

Unit 07

• Reading Skill • Using Context Clues

A context clue is a hint or a source of information that helps the reader understand the meaning of a word. It is used to give assistance to the meaning of the word. This can be done directly or indirectly.

Build up the Skill

Types of Context Clues	
Synonyms	The day seemed to be idyllic. It was peaceful and calm. It was a nearly perfect day for walking outside.
Antonyms	She is a famous star in her country but unknown to the rest of the world.
Definitions	There is a 30 percent chance of precipitation, such as snow or sleet.
Explanations	The cat has a kind disposition and would never bite or claw anyone.
Comparisons	The trip to Japan was better my expedition to Africa.
Contrasts	The photo of the landscape is picturesque, but the one of the old houses is ugly.

1. Identify the correct type of context clues for each sentence.

1. Marty is sociable, not like his brother who is quiet and shy. _____
2. She taps the desk continuously, by making a regular sound. _____
3. Some astronomic bodies, such as the planets and stars, can be seen with the naked eye. _____
4. When the hammer hit his thumb, he winced in pain and kept flinched. _____
5. Eating nutritious food is just as important as regular exercise. _____
6. The cool weather was a welcome relief from the sweltering heat of summer. _____

2. Choose the correct meaning of the words based on context clues.

1. I have a difficult conundrum or puzzle to solve.
   a. quiz   b. mystery   c. test   d. book

2. Many people in the country live in poverty even though there is great prosperity in the country.
   a. proof   b. people   c. wealth   d. health

3. The refrigerator has a putrid odor inside; the rotten smell escaped when the door was opened.
   a. bad   **b.** good   **c.** fragrant   **d.** aromatic

• Writing • I Always Take a Shower in the Morning

1. Pre-writing Answer the following questions to prepare to write.

- What is your daily routine?
- What do you usually do in the morning?
- When do you bathe or take a shower?
- Name something that you rarely do.
- What is something you never do at night?

2. Writing the First Draft Write about your daily routine. Use the answers from the Pre-writing activity to organize your writing. Focus on the sequence of the events.

> **Example** My alarm always wakes me up at the same time each day. I get up and wash my face. I don't have to wash my hair in the morning because I frequently take a shower at night. I never eat breakfast, but I usually eat lunch around noon. Sometimes I take a nap in the afternoon. I regularly take a shower after I exercise and before I go to bed. I never eat right before I go to sleep.

3. Peer Review Exchange your writing with a partner. Then read your partner's writing and look for mistakes or errors. Make corrections on them and return the writing to your partner.

4. Rewriting Look at the corrections that your partner made and revise your writing based on the corrections. Try to rewrite the parts you'd like to change in order to improve your writing.

Unit 08

• Reading Skill • Making Inferences

An Inference is an assumption or a conclusion that is made based on the given facts. When reading, we make inferences by assuming the author's purpose and relating ourselves to the text.

Build up the Skill

Read the paragraphs and answer the questions.

> "Achoo!" Laura sneezed for the third time. She then sneezed again and again. Her head started to hurt and she felt very warm. Laura dragged herself out of bed long enough to make a call to her boss. The boss answered the phone, and she said that she couldn't go to work today.

1. Why wasn't Laura going to work?

_____

2. What clues or hints from the paragraph helped you to make this inference?

_____

> Amy ran out of the bathroom. She had tears welling in her eyes as she found her way to the cafeteria. She asked the staff if they had any rice she could have. They had some to give her in a red plastic cup. Amy thanked them as she pulled out her phone and put it into the cup of rice. Fortunately, the rice was dry, but Amy telephone was still damp after she dropped it in the bathroom. She thanked the staff went back to class. She was relieved, but she still felt more than a little worried.

3. Why did Amy have tears in her eyes at the beginning of the paragraph?

_____

4. Why did Amy put her phone in the cup of rice?

_____

5. Why was Amy relieved but still worried at the end of the paragraph?

_____

> Troy put the finishing touches on his car's fender. He moved his cloth in circular patterns as he wiped and polished his car's paint. He took great care of his car. It wasn't a race car, but he was very proud of his car because he had paid for it himself. He put down the chamois after wiping down the trunk and bumper. He stepped back from his work

and admired all that he had done. The car shined and looked amazing. All of a sudden there was a crack of thunder. He looked over his shoulder to see storm clouds rolling in. He got so mad, so he kicked over the water bucket.

6. What was Troy doing?

7. Why did Troy get mad at the end?

• Writing • May I Have Time Off?

1. **Pre-writing** Answer the following questions to prepare to write.

   Imagine that you're working for a company and want to take some time off.
   - When would you like to take a vacation?
   - Why do you need to take time off?
   - Where would you like to go?
   - Will you be leaving the country?
   - How long will you be away?

2. **Writing the First Draft** Write an email to ask your supervisor or boss for time off. Use the answers from the Pre-writing activity to organize your writing.

   > Example
   >
   > To: mr.manager@pagoda.com
   >
   > Dear Manager,
   >
   > I am writing to request a two-week vacation at the beginning of September; beginning on September 2nd and finishing on September 15th. My brother will be getting married on the 7th, and he has asked me to be his best man. I am submitting my request 6 months in advance to secure the week before and after his wedding as vacation time. Please let me know at your earliest convenience.
   >
   > Sincerely,
   >
   > Richard Lewis

3. **Peer Review** Exchange your writing with a partner. Then read your partner's writing and look for mistakes or errors. Make corrections on them and return the writing to your partner.

4. **Rewriting** Look at the corrections that your partner made and revise your writing based on the corrections. Try to rewrite the parts you'd like to change in order to improve your writing.

Unit 09

• Reading Skill • Cause and Effect

A cause is an event or an action that makes something happen. To find the cause, ask yourself why this happened.

effect is what happens as a result of the cause. To find an effect, ask yourself what happened in that part of the story.

Build up the Skill

Read the paragraphs and answer the questions.

> A seed falls from a tree. Rain soaks it and the Sun warms it. Roots grow. The seeds grow into a new plant!

1. Why do roots grow?

2. What do the seeds grow into?

> Jim was fishing at the pond. He had a rod with a hook. He forgot the worms. He couldn't catch a fish.

3. What happened when Jim went fishing?

4. Why didn't Jim catch a fish?

> My feet were hot. I took off my shoes and socks. Then, I felt better.

5. Why did the writer take off his shoes?

6. Why did the writer's feet feel better?

It is a widely believed superstition that going out in cold weather will make you sick, especially, if you are improperly dressed. However, the temperature is not what causes you to get sick. Illnesses are caused by germs and not by standing in the cold shivering. Standing outside in the cold with little protection won't strengthen your immune system and you are more likely to get sick indoors. This is mainly due to a greater exposure to germs.

7. Why do many people get sick by going out in cold weather?
   _____

8. Illnesses are caused by _____ not _____ .

• Writing • I Totally Recommend That You Go to That Restaurant!

1. **Pre-writing** Answer the following questions to prepare to write.

   Imagine that you're at one of your favorite restaurants.
   - What does the restaurant look like?
   - What kind of food do they serve?
   - Where is it located?
   - Are there any special foods or items on the menu?
   - What would you like to recommend?

2. **Writing the First Draft** Write an introduction of one of your favorite restaurants. Use the answers from the Pre-writing activity to organize your writing.

   Example Be sure not to stuff yourself with the amazing food and save some room for dessert. When you are at the Nick's restaurant for a real treat, I highly recommend the tiramisu. It is to do for. Most nights the place is packed with people, but you might get lucky and actually meet Nick himself. If you are ever in the area and feel like having some great Italian food, I recommend that you stop by Nick's.

3. **Peer Review** Exchange your writing with a partner. Then read your partner's writing and look for mistakes or errors. Make corrections on them and return the writing to your partner.

4. **Rewriting** Look at the corrections that your partner made and revise your writing based on the corrections. Try to rewrite the parts you'd like to change in order to improve your writing.

Unit 10

• Reading Skill • Summary

A summary is a short version of a longer source of material. The main goal is to present the most important ideas from the original material in a short and easy way to follow text.

* How to produce a summary:

1. Read the article, book, or other material that is to be summarized. Make sure you understand it.
2. Outline the article. Make note of major points and important information.
3. Write the first draft without looking at the article, book, or other material.
4. Always paraphrase in a summary. If you copy a phrase or a passage from the original, be very sure to put quotation marks around it. You should only copy if the phrase or the passage is necessary and cannot or should not be paraphrased.
5. The target length for the first draft of the summary should be approximately ¼ the length of the original article, book, or other material.

▤ Build up the Skill

Summarize the paragraphs.

> Frogs and toads belong to a class of animals called amphibians which were among the animals to leave the sea and inhabit for the surface of the earth.

1. _____

> Steady increase in the number of the private ownership of petrol or diesel vehicles is one of the most obvious phenomena to plague big cities like New York. It fills the roads and renders rapid movement more difficult with other public transportation.

2. _____

> People whose professional activities lie in the field of politics are not, on the whole, known for their respect for factual accuracy.

3. _____

> Failure to eat a sufficient quantity of solid food over an extended period of time will certainly lead to fatal consequences.

4. _____

> A large majority of non-native learners of English experience an unquestionable number of problems struggling to master the sound patterns of the language.

5. _____

> The climate conditions found in the tropical island show a pattern of irregular and unpredictable periods of dry and wet weather, which goes along with a similarly irregular cycle of temperature changes.

6. _____

• Writing • How Do You Keep Yourself So Healthy?

1. Pre-writing Answer the following questions to prepare to write.

- How often do you exercise: daily, twice a week, or three times a week?
- Do you take vitamins or health supplements?
- Do you routinely visit your doctor for a check-up even if you are not sick?
- How many hours do you normally sleep?
- What would you like to do for your health?

2. Writing the First Draft Write about your healthy and unhealthy habits. Use the answers from the Pre-writing activity to organize your writing.

> **Example** "I'm too busy to exercise." It's an excuse that I say too often. I'm busy, but I should make time to exercise at least a little bit every day. I do take vitamin supplements to help keep my body healthy. Trying to start a career is difficult on a person's body. I work long hours and don't eat very well. I get 4-5 hours of sleep a night, but hopefully after my next promotion I will be able to rest more.

3. Peer Review Exchange your writing with a partner. Then read your partner's writing and look for mistakes or errors. Make corrections on them and return the writing to your partner.

4. Rewriting Look at the corrections that your partner made and revise your writing based on the corrections. Try to rewrite the parts you'd like to change in order to improve your writing.

Unit 11

• Reading Skill • Identifying Pronoun References

> **A pronoun** should clearly refer to one unmistakable noun that precedes the pronoun. That noun is referred to as the *pronoun's antecedent*.
> **General pronoun reference** - the use of a pronoun that refers to a general idea rather than a specific antecedent to rephrase the sentence or to replace a noun with the pronoun
> **Weak pronoun reference** - the use of pronoun which refers to an antecedent that has been suggested but not expressed

Build up the Skill

What do the bolded pronouns refer to?

> Mariana told jokes and sang funny songs. **This** amused her audience.
> → **This** means Mariana's act, telling jokes and singing funny songs.

1. My family got new carpet and curtains. **That** certainly improved the room's appearance.
   → **That** means _____.

2. The people want the public servants to be honest, but more often than not, people think that **it** is not a virtue held by any of the candidates.
   → The antecedent of **it** is _____. It is suggested, but not expressed.

3. The hiking trail was covered in boulders, debris, and washed out in places. **It** made the climb more difficult than usual.
   → **It** means that _____.

4. Being neighborly is important because you may need **their** help someday in an emergency.
   → The antecedent of **their** is _____. It is suggested but not expressed.

5. Mark called Mary's house all day, but **she** never answered the phone.
   → The antecedent of **she** is _____.

6. More than half of the trees in the park had to be cut down, **which** was unfortunate.
   → **Which** refers to that _____.

7. The limousine turned sharply to the right when **it** passed the bus.

   → **It** means _____.

8. Last Saturday, we pulled weeds in the garden, but **it** took longer than we had planned.

   → **It** means that _____.

• Writing • Do You Have Time To Meet on Monday?

1. Pre-writing Answer the following questions to prepare to write.

> Imagine you're writing a message to request a meeting.
> - Who are you sending the request to?
> - What business are you going to discuss?
> - Why do you need to meet?
> - When do you have free time?
> - Where would you like to meet?

2. Writing the First Draft Write a message to someone to request a meeting. Use the answers from the Pre-writing activity to organize your writing.

> **Example**
>
> To Mr. Bigwig,
>
> I would like to have a meeting with you sometime in the next week. We need to discuss some of our products and how they are not functioning as they should. I have a busy schedule next week, but I have free time on Tuesday, Wednesday, and Friday in the afternoon. Please send me a message and let me know which day and time is best for you.
>
> Thank you.

3. Peer Review Exchange your writing with a partner. Then read your partner's writing and look for mistakes or errors. Make corrections on them and return the writing to your partner.

4. Rewriting Look at the corrections that your partner made and revise your writing based on the corrections. Try to rewrite the parts you'd like to change in order to improve your writing.

Unit 12

• Reading Skill • Finding Supporting Details

Finding supporting details is to take a large selection of text and reduce it to the main points for more concise understanding.

Build up the Skill

Read the following passages. Each consists of a main idea and several details. Choose the correct answers to the questions.

> The generational group called the Millennials consists mainly of students who were born after 1982. This group tends to exhibit very different characteristics from those students who were born only a few years earlier. Among the differences are these:
> They prefer group activities.
> They tend to spend more time doing homework and housework or chores.
> They spend less time watching the television.
> They believe it's cool to be smart.
> They are fascinated by new technologies.

1. **Which of the following can be supporting details for the passage?** _____, _____, _____
   a. Students born after 1982 are considered Millennials, and they exhibit quite different characteristics from those of students only a few years older.
   b. They tend to spend more time doing homework and housework or chores.
   c. They spend less time watching the television.
   d. They are fascinated by new technologies.

2. **What do the major details of the passage tell us?**
   a. an explanation of how the term Millennial came about
   b. characteristics of Millennials
   c. the process of becoming a Millennial
   d. the belief that it's cool to be smart

> Before smartphones were all the rage, PDAs were the go-to electronic device. Personal Digital Assistants were hand-held electronic organizers that were small and easy to carry. The prices and capabilities of these mini computers varied. They were usually operated by using a special pen called a stylus. PDAs were the predecessor to modern smart phones. Some of the cheapest and most basic of them were monochromatic. These devices were used to store and collect information such as names, phone numbers, email addresses, etc. Some of the more expensive models had color screens and offered more computer-like programs. A few had the ability to manage your email accounts and create documents. Some even had calendar

functions that would allow you to keep track of your appointments and special events. A few of the newer PDAs even had the ability to play video or audio files. The most expensive ones offered phone and text messaging functions. Today's smartphones owe an awful lot to the PDAs.

3. **Which of the following are supporting details in the passage?** _____, _____, _____
   a. Personal Digital Assistants were hand-held electronic organizers that were small and easy to carry.
   b. More expensive models had color screens and offered computer-like applications.
   c. The most expensive ones offered phone and text messaging functions.
   d. A few of the newer PDAs even had the ability to play video or audio files.

4. **The purpose of the details in this passage is** _____.
   a. to give reasons to buy a color PDA
   b. to explain differences between inexpensive and expensive PDAs
   c. to show the procedure for buying a PDA
   d. to describe various capabilities of PDAs

• Writing • Are You Looking for a Roommate?

1. **Pre-writing** Answer the following questions to prepare to write.

   Imagine you're writing an ad to look for a new roommate.
   - What kind of person do you want to live with?
   - Where are you located?
   - How much rent do you pay a month? / How much should your roommate pay a month?
   - What habits can you live with? / What can you not live with?
   - Are there any restrictions for you or your roommate?

2. **Writing the First Draft** Write a blog or newspaper ad looking for a new roommate. Use the answers from the Pre-writing activity to organize your writing.

   > **Example** Are you looking for a new place to live? Well, I have a room available for rent. I am located near downtown in a safe apartment building. Rent is $500 plus half of the utilities a month. No pets allowed - I have allergies. I am a night person, so I usually stay up most of the night. I don't mind smoking, but please do it outside. If you are interested, please call 123-2345-0000.

3. **Peer Review** Exchange your writing with a partner. Then read your partner's writing and look for mistakes or errors. Make corrections on them and return the writing to your partner.

4. **Rewriting** Look at the corrections that your partner made and revise your writing based on the corrections. Try to rewrite the parts you'd like to change in order to improve your writing.

Script

Unit 01 | Script

Vocabulary

1. I know Tony, but not very well. He is one of my acquaintances.
2. Paul is working with me. He is my colleague.
3. My boss, Richard, is very kind. Everyone likes his leadership.
4. Nick was one of my classmates when I was a high school student.
5. Veronica is one of my relatives. She is my cousin.
6. Henry and I have dated for three years. I am so happy to have him as my boyfriend.
7. I tell everything to Timothy. He is my best friend.
8. Jane lives next door. She is not a picky neighbor.

Conversation

Thom: Wow! Where did you take this picture?
Laura: Oh, I went to Europe with my best friend.
Thom: Really? I went to see the Sistine Chapel two years ago.
Laura: I didn't get to see that, but my parents did.
Thom: What about this picture?
Laura: My boyfriend and I went scuba diving in the Caribbean in July.
Thom: My colleagues and I are planning to do that next year.
Laura: It will be fun. Ah, here is my favorite picture!

Listen Up

1. Getting Ready

a. Mary talked with her neighbor, Kim.
b. Kai went to the amusement park with his girlfriend, Devon.
c. Bobby got up to a little mischief with his friend, Charlie.
d. Winona went on a business trip with her co-worker, Michael.

2. Easy Listening

Man: Is my hotel reservation for next week made?
Woman: Of course. I made the reservation last week and confirmed it this morning.
Man: And, how about my flight? Were you able to change it to a later time?
Woman: No, all the later flights were booked.
Man: Oh, that's too bad… And is my suit at the dry cleaners?
Woman: Yes, you can pick it up on your way home tonight.
Man: That's good. Well, let's get to work so I can leave tomorrow.

3. Hard Rock

John: Hey, William! How was your holiday?
William: It was great. I had so much fun on this holiday.
John: Really? What did you do?
William: I went to an amusement park with my girlfriend. Then I went my hometown to visit my relatives. And I hung out with my best friend, Rick.
John: Rick from your high school?
William: Oh, yeah. And we got into some mischief with a few acquaintances of his.
John: Haha. It sounds like you really enjoyed your holiday.
William: How about you? What did you do?
John: Well, I just spent time at home, relaxing and playing video games.

Unit 02 | Script

Conversation

Alice: Happy Birthday, Daehan!
Daehan: You remembered! Thank you so much.
Alice: Why wouldn't I remember?
Daehan: Last year, it was on Easter Sunday. So, most

of my friends forgot my birthday.

Alice: Really? Does your birthday usually fall on the same day as Easter?

Daehan: No, that was the second time Easter and my birthday were on the same day.

Alice: You're lucky. My birthday is always on a holiday.

Daehan: I know your birthday is in the winter. Is it on New Year's Day?

Alice: Nope, my birthday is on Christmas day.

Listen Up

1. Getting Ready

1. My Parent's wedding anniversary is on November 12th.
2. July 22nd is Julius's house warming party.
3. Easter is at the end of March.
4. We have Halloween on October 31st.

2. Easy Listening

Michael: Hey, Carrie! Did you hear that there will be a costume party at Freddie's on Saturday?

Carrie: Yeah, I did. But I'm not sure when it begins.

Michael: It's supposed to start at 10.

Carrie: Let's meet at 9:30 and go together.

Michael: Sounds good. It should be a great Halloween party.

Carrie: I think I'm going to dress up as a witch. What's your costume, Michael?

Michael: Something simple, maybe a ghost or Dracula.

Carrie: I heard that Freddie's going to be Frankenstein.

Michael: I can hardly wait until Saturday.

3. Hard Rock

Woman: Did you get some roses for your girlfriend?

Man: Oh, no! I totally forgot about it.

Woman: You told me to remind you. It's your one year anniversary today.

Man: Ugh... Right. I need to make a dinner reservation.

Woman: I actually did that for you. The restaurant is expecting you at 7:30.

Man: Oh, thank you. You are the greatest friend. Do you know where I can buy some roses?

Woman: There is a flower shop across the street.

Man: You just saved my life and my relationship.

Woman: That's okay. Your girlfriend is my friend after all.

Unit 03 | Script

Conversation

Doug: Annie, would you like to go on a picnic tomorrow?

Annie: Sounds like fun.

Doug: I know a great place near the lake.

Annie: Hum... Should I bring my bathing suit?

Doug: Sure, we could do some sunbathing, or maybe even water-skiing.

Annie: Oh, I love waterskiing. But I've lost my bathing suit.

Doug: Umm... Okay, then I have the best idea. Why don't we fly a kite?

Annie: No, I don't like those small kites.

Doug: I was thinking of the bigger ones.

Annie: Well, while you are flying your kite, I'll just pick some flowers.

Listen Up

2. Easy Listening

Man: Wow, look! It's the first snow of the year.

Woman: Oh great. We can go snowboarding next weekend.

Man: Snowboarding is too hard for me. Skiing is much easier.

Woman: Skiing is not as hard as snowboarding. You can ski while I snowboard then.

Man: I like that idea. Let's go outside now and build a snowman.

Woman: I don't know if there is enough snow yet.

Man: We'll just have to wait until the snow piles up then.

3. Hard Rock

Woman: Tonight is the big night for the astronomy club.
Man: I'm so excited. It's the longest night of the year.
Woman: And the sky is as clear as crystal. It's perfect weather.
Man: What are you going to look at tonight?
Woman: I can't wait to see Jupiter with my own eyes.
Man: What do you mean? You can see it most nights.
Woman: I know it's the third brightest thing in the night sky. But today it's as close as it is ever possible.
Man: Well, let's go now. Maybe we can look at the Moon before it sets.
Woman: We'd better bundle up before we go. It's cold outside. Bring your coat and gloves.
Man: I will. Don't forget some coffee and hot cocoa.

Review Units 01~03

Conversation

Laura: Hey, Doug. Do you have any plans for your Thanksgiving holiday?
Doug: Annie and I are planning to visit my parents and her relatives.
Laura: Wow, that sounds like a lot of traveling.
Doug: It is, but it's always good to go home. How about your plans?
Laura: Well, my boyfriend and I are going to celebrate our one year anniversary.
Doug: Has it been a year already?
Laura: Yep. We met on the field day.
Doug: I forgot that you went to school together.
Laura: Yes, we did. And I'm planning a picnic for us after the actual holiday.
Doug: Aren't you going to visit your hometown?
Laura: I can't. I have to work at my part-time job.
Doug: Oh, no! Didn't your boss give you the day off?
Laura: No, but that's okay. I'm making extra money for Daehan's present.

Unit 04 | Script

Conversation

Alex: How are you going to go home for Thanksgiving?
Mary: I have a ticket for a flight at seven tonight.
Alex: I heard that there is going to be a snowstorm later today. You may want to change to the train like I did.
Mary: Oh, no! A snowstorm could cancel all the flights.
Alex: You should come with me on the train most of the way.
Mary: Most of the way? Then what?
Alex: We can rent a car or take a bus.
Mary: Renting a car sounds better than taking a bus.
Alex: Call the airline and cancel your ticket first. Then later, I'll call a taxi to go to the station.

Listen Up

1. Getting Ready

1. Marcus's brother has hired a limousine to take Marcus to his home for the holidays.
2. Elizabeth is trying to save money, so she takes the bus home for Thanksgiving.
3. Catherine and her boyfriend are taking a romantic train ride to meet their parents.
4. Daniel has to get home quickly by airplane.

2. Easy Listening

Man: Look! They're going to offer free tickets for the maglev train next week.
Woman: I hate trains. they're too noisy.
Man: This one isn't.
Woman: I thought it was like a subway train.
Man: No, this is a special train. It floats on magnets.
Woman: Oh, that sounds interesting.
Man: Should we try getting the tickets?
Woman: Yes, let's do it.

3. Hard Rock

Man: Are you ready for next week's trip?
Woman: Oh yeah, I have made some great travel plans.

Man: What is it?
Woman: Well, my friend and I are going to take a train first. And then we'll bike around the country for five days.
Man: That sounds fun.
Woman: I'll call you as often as I can.
Man: Good. I don't want anything bad to happen to you.
Woman: Don't worry. We'll be fine.
Man: I remember your bike trip three years ago.
Woman: Yeah, me too. Accidents do happen.
Man: Just be careful.

Unit 05 | Script

Conversation

Rick: Let's make stew. Do we have celery, onions, and cabbage?
Emily: Yes, but we need more.
Rick: Then I'll go buy some. What else do we have in the fridge?
Emily: We have chicken, pork, and salmon.
Rick: We can use the pork, but beef always tastes better.
Emily: Okay. Do we need anything else?
Rick: We need some butter, a loaf of bread, and some olive oil.
Emily: Oh, some cheese and wine would be good, too.
Rick: Right, I will go to the store now.
Emily: Okay! See you when you get back.

Listen Up

1. Getting Ready
- Cindy is going on a picnic tomorrow and wants to bring sandwiches.
- Jerry is making a cake for his girlfriend's birthday.
- Rachel wants to have a sweet vanilla ice-cream sundae for dessert.

2. Easy Listening
Child: Mom, can we buy some cookies?
Mom: No, sorry we can't today. How about some carrots?
Child: I don't like carrots. They hurt my braces.
Mom: Ok, then why don't you go get some milk for us?
Child: Can I get chocolate milk?
Mom: Yes, but only a small one. Get some regular milk, too.
Child: That's too heavy. I can't carry it.
Mom: Yes, you can.
Child: Okay, I'll be right back.

3. Hard Rock
Clerk: May I help you?
Customer: Yes, I need some fresh beef, please.
Clerk: And how much would you like?
Customer: I need 4 pounds.
Clerk: Would you like the steak or stew meat?
Customer: What's the price difference?
Clerk: The steak is $13 and the stew meat is $6 per pound.
Customer: Let me have half and half: 2 pounds each.
Clerk: Here you go. Anything else?
Customer: Um… Where are the dairy products?
Clerk: They're in the back of the store.
Customer: Thank you.

Unit 06 | Script

Conversation

Eileen: Oh, no! Were you in another car accident?
Jerry: Well, yes. But this time, it wasn't my fault.
Eileen: Okay, what happened?
Jerry: I was driving on a highway and a car bumped mine.
Eileen: Didn't you see the driver?
Jerry: Yes, I did. He just didn't see me.
Eileen: How bad was the damage?
Jerry: Not bad. Just some minor damage and scratches, but he drove away before I could get out of my car.
Eileen: You mean a hit and run?
Jerry: Yes, so I called the police and the insurance company.

Listen Up

2. Easy Listening

Jennifer: Rachel! What happened to your arm?
Rachel: Oh, my cat Garfield scratched me… But, I'm okay.
Jennifer: Why would Garfield do that to you?
Rachel: My boyfriend James and I were trying to give him a bath.
Jennifer: I see, he has always hated getting bathed.
Rachel: Yes, like the other cats… I feel bad for James.
Jennifer: Why? What happened to him?
Rachel: While Garfield was scratching me, he was biting James's chest.
Jennifer: Really? Is he okay?
Rachel: Garfield or James?
Jennifer: Um.. Both of them.

3. Hard Rock

Officer: May I see your driver's license and proof of insurance, please?
Man: Just a moment. Here they are.
Officer: Did you know you were driving with an expired license?
Man: Uh… yes… I renewed it last week. But it hasn't arrived yet.
Officer: Do you know why I pulled you over?
Man: Not really.
Officer: You were going 60mph in a 30mph zone.
Man: Really? But I didn't see the speed limit sign.
Officer: With that and the expired license, I'm going to write you two tickets.

Review Units 04~06

Conversation

Steve: Leigh, may I borrow your bicycle?
Leigh: Sorry, it has a flat tire. What happened to yours?
Steve: It had a slight accident last night.
Leigh: What happened?
Steve: Well, last night I went to get some beef and cheese at a grocery store.
Leigh: I remember. We had cheeseburgers together with Del at your home last night.
Steve: Well, I locked up my bike downstairs like usual.
Leigh: Of course. What happened next?
Steve: When Del left, he must have put his car in reverse instead of drive.
Leigh: Oh no, did he run over your bike?
Steve: Yep, he caused some minor damage. Oh, well. I guess I'd better call a taxi to get to work.
Leigh: When Rick comes home, we'll take your bike in his truck to the repair shop.
Steve: Thanks.

Unit 07 | Script

Conversation

Shannon: What are you wearing on your date, Rachel?
Rachel: I don't know. I never have anything to wear.
Shannon: What about this red dress?
Rachel: Oh, I usually wear that one to work.
Shannon: Well, how about this outfit? You hardly ever wear it.
Rachel: That outfit is so out of style. Ugh! Can I borrow some of your clothes?
Shannon: But I rarely get my things back from you.
Rachel: What do you mean? I always return your stuff.
Shannon: Really? What about this blue dress?
Rachel: Well, occasionally, I forget.

Listen Up

1. Getting Ready

- Laura occasionally brushes her teeth with her daughter.
- John generally shaves in the morning before work.
- Daniel drinks tea in the afternoon all the time.
- Alice hardly ever takes a shower in the morning.

2. Easy Listening

Woman: You look so tired. What's happening?
Man: I always look tired. I work three jobs.
Woman: Don't you ever have free time?
Man: I do, but not too often. If I'm not working, I'm sleeping.
Woman: You must be making a lot of money.

Man: It's never enough to pay all the bills.
Woman: What kind of bills are you talking about?
Man: I'm paying off my student loans and credit card bills.
Woman: Oh, that must be rough.

3. Hard Rock
Woman: Why are all of the baseball team players wearing armbands?
Man: Oh, they are trying to raise money for a good cause.
Woman: I see. They are always trying to do something good for others.
Man: Yeah, they usually help charities and individuals.
Woman: So that's why they occasionally have the pre-game activities.
Man: That's right. Why don't we go down and make a donation?
Woman: That sounds like a good idea. I have $20.
Man: And I have $35, so we can donate $55 to help.
Woman: It always feels great to help others.

Unit 08 | Script

Conversation
Kara: May I see your airline ticket, sir?
Paul: Sure, here you are.
Kara: Thank you. You will be in seat 33C in economy class.
Paul: Is that an aisle seat?
Kara: Yes, it is also an exit row seat. Here is your boarding pass.
Paul: Thank you.
Kara: Excuse me, Sir. May I see your luggage?
Paul: Is there a problem?
Kara: It is too large for the overhead bins. Your suitcase must be checked in.
Paul: Alright, but please waive the baggage fee.

Listen Up

1. Getting Ready
- Christina is supposed to attend a meeting in Hong Kong on September 3rd. She'll travel by airplane.
- Fredrick is scheduled to take the bus to Washington D.C. on July 3rd.
- Peter's train leaves for Milan on January 25th. His return is the next day.

2. Easy Listening
Travel Agent: We have two different travel packages you might be interested in.
Woman: Which one would be cheaper?
Travel Agent: That would be the five-day simple package.
Woman: Would you tell me about the other one?
Travel Agent: Our second option is the seven-day package, and you'll be much more comfortable.
Woman: I think I would rather take the first one.
Travel Agent: Alright, would you like to make any upgrades like sauna trip, queen size bed, or room with a view?
Woman: No thanks, just the basic package.
Travel Agent: Alright, let's get the reservation made.

3. Hard Rock
Man: Hello, I need to book a flight to Paris for Saturday morning.
Woman: Yes, sir. Would you prefer a non-stop flight or one with a layover?
Man: I think the non-stop is better.
Woman: Very well. We have flights leaving at 7:30 and 8:50.
Man: I would rather take the 8:50 flight. Which one has seats with more leg room?
Woman: The 7:30 has more space available.
Man: I will take a ticket on the 7:30 flight then.
Woman: Okay. Please be sure to arrive at least an hour early to check-in.
Man: Of course. How long will it take to get through security?
Woman: It usually takes about half an hour. So give yourself enough time.
Man: I will, thank you.

Unit 09 | Script

Conversation

Jennifer: Would you tell me what today's specials are?
Eric: Certainly. Our set menu begins with a starter of soup or salad.
Jennifer: What kind of soup is it?
Eric: Today, it is broccoli cheese or potato bacon.
Jennifer: And what is the main dish?
Eric: We have a beef steak or chicken breast served in wine sauce. All dishes are followed by dessert.
Jennifer: I'm on a diet. Can the dessert be changed to coffee?
Eric: Of course. Would you like to try today's special?
Jennifer: Yes, I would like the beef steak and salad with the coffee for dessert.
Eric: Very good. Let me put in your order.

Listen Up

1. Getting Ready

- Charles is going to have the chicken with potatoes and peas.
- Daniel wants to eat a light salad.
- Annie is craving for some grilled fish.
- Doug wants a big hamburger and some french fries.

2. Easy Listening

Man: Excuse me, I'm next in line.
Woman: Oh, I'm sorry. I didn't see you. Would it be okay if I order first? I'm running late.
Man: Since you asked so politely, go right ahead.
Woman: Thank you so much. (To the waiter) I need to place three orders to go, and I want to pay for this man's order as well.
Waiter: OK, would you like it in separate bags?
Woman: Yes, please.
Man: You don't have to pay for my order. I would prefer to pay for my own.
Woman: You were very kind, so I want to thank you.

3. Hard Rock

Staff: Ladies and gentlemen, we're looking for two volunteers to take a later flight.
Woman: I would rather take the later flight if that is ok with you.
Man: We can't really take it. We need to be in the office early tomorrow.
Woman: They might give us something special.
Man: Hmm... True, and we could always sleep on the flight.
Woman: We'll take the later flight. Is there anything special we can get?
Staff: Yes, ma'am. Would you like to upgrade your tickets to first class or get a voucher for an upgrade on your next flight?
Man: I think that I'd like to upgrade this flight.
Woman: Me too. I've never been in first class.
Man: Me neither.
Staff: Alright, here are your new boarding passes. We begin boarding at 10:15 p.m.

Review Units 07~09

Conversation

Rachel: These seats are not that comfortable.
Avion: They never are in economy class.
Rachel: I can't believe this is a non-stop flight. I know I'll get airsickness.
Avion: Don't worry. You can usually walk around a little during the flight.
Rachel: Good to know. I'm getting hungry. Is there anything we can eat?
Avion: We get a meal during the flight. Will you get the chicken or beef?
Rachel: I'll try the chicken. What about you?
Avion: I wonder if they have a vegan option.
Rachel: I think they do. I forgot you don't like to eat meat.
Avion: Well, occasionally I try a little bit.
Rachel: Look at the menu in the seat pocket.
Avion: Oh good! They do have an option without meat!
Rachel: At least this airline has food on it.
Avion: Yeah. Makes up for the uncomfortable seats.

Unit 10 | Script

Conversation

Veronica: Are you feeling any better, Charles?
Charles: Not really, I still have a fever, and I'm still nauseous.
Veronica: Did you take the medicine the doctor gave you?
Charles: No, I forgot to get the prescription filled.
Veronica: You'll never get better if you don't take it.
Charles: You're right. Would you go to the pharmacy for me?
Veronica: Sure, I need your insurance card and the prescription.
Charles: Here they are. Thanks, Veronica.
Veronica: I'll be back in an hour. Rest. You look exhausted.
Charles: Okay. I will.

Listen Up

2. Easy Listening

Woman: What is that you're eating?
Man: It's a hot dog. Do you want some?
Woman: Are you kidding? Do you know what's in that?
Man: Not really, it just tastes good.
Woman: If you knew what is in there, you wouldn't eat that.
Man: Well, what should I eat?
Woman: You should eat more vegetables and fruits.
Man: OK, maybe I could make a banana hot dog…
Woman: It's your life, but they say you are what you eat.

3. Hard Rock

Man: Aren't you going to stretch before you exercise?
Woman: Not really, I'm only doing a light workout today.
Man: You're careless. You should always stretch first.
Woman: Well, could you show me how to do it?
Man: First you start with your neck and slowly work your way down to your toes.
Woman: Okay, do you have any other tips to help me?
Man: What are you drinking while working out?
Woman: I have some sports drink in a bottle.
Man: That's the worst thing for your health.
Woman: What should I be drinking?
Man: Water is always the best for your health.

Unit 11 | Script

Conversation

Joy: Can you help me with this?
Sam: Sure, what's up?
Joy: I need to send a reply to make an appointment on behalf of my boss by email. Can you look at it first?
Sam: Of course. Send it to me.
Joy: I already did. Check your inbox.
Sam: I don't see it. Let me check my spam folder… Got it.
Joy: So, what do you think?
Sam: It's not bad. But let me highlight the parts you should delete. And you shouldn't use emoticons. They look unprofessional.
Joy: Thanks, I'll edit and send it. And I'll CC you on the message.
Sam: Make it BCC. I don't want the boss to know I'm helping you.
Joy: Will do. Thanks again.

Listen Up

2. Easy Listening

Man: Did you give my number to Maryann?
Woman: Yes. She asked me if I had it.
Man: Please let me know next time.
Woman: I'm sorry. Did I make a mistake?
Man: Well, yes. Actually, you made a huge one.
Woman: I don't understand.
Man: I changed my number so Maryann would stop calling me.
Woman: So, giving her your number ruined everything.
Man: Please, don't give out my number to other people.
Woman: I promise. I won't let anyone else have it.

3. Hard Rock

Woman: Thank you for calling customer support team. How may I help you?
Man: Yes, I received a package yesterday from your company.
Woman: Would you please give me your name?
Man: Charles Bucket…B U C K E T…
Woman: Yes, Mr. Bucket, we had your package delivered to your house yesterday at three o'clock.
Man: That's right. But the problem is that it's the wrong package.
Woman: Let me have the product number, please.
Man: It's B5317-A249, but I ordered the B5317-4249.
Woman: I see the problem. We'll ship the right part to you today. I'm sorry for the inconvenience.
Man: Thank you, and have a nice day.

Unit 12 | Script

Conversation

Daniel: Excuse me. Could you tell me how to get to the College of Engineering?
Holli: Sure. Go up this road until you see the Student Union building.
Daniel: Where do I go from there?
Holli: The engineering building is right next to it.
Daniel: How much time will it take?
Holli: It's going to take you about 10 minutes.
Daniel: Can you show me where we are on the campus map?
Holli: Sure, we are here and this is the library.
Daniel: I see where I am. Thanks.

Listen Up

1. Getting Ready

a. I have $25 to spend on the present.
b. I'd like to add some candies on it.
c. Yes, I would like to buy something for my friend.
d. It will be ready after 3:20.

2. Easy Listening

Man: Hello, I'd like to order a cake for a birthday.
Woman: What kind of cake would you like?
Man: I'm thinking about a chocolate cake with white icing.
Woman: We can do that. What would you like it to say?
Man: "Happy Birthday, Victoria!" What else can you put on the cake?
Woman: We can add flowers, candies, swirls, or shells.
Man: Could you put red and blue flowers on it?
Woman: Certainly, when would you like to pick it up?
Man: I'm working until 4:30. How about 5 o'clock?
Woman: Okay. We'll have it ready for you.

3. Hard Rock

Woman: Hello. I'm looking for a special present for someone.
Man: Well, we have a whole selection of special items right here.
Woman: I only have 25 dollars to spend.
Man: We're having a special on these items here.
Woman: These are a little too childish. Do you have anything more sophisticated?
Man: How about this? It's in your price range and for an adult.
Woman: Do you have different colors?
Man: I'm afraid this is the only color we have right now.
Woman: Oh, that's too bad. I was looking forward to buying it.
Man: Hold on. Let me call the other store and see if they have different colors.

Review Units 10~12

Conversation

Cindy: Are you okay, Daniel?

Daniel: Not really, my leg hurts.

Cindy: Why were you in such a hurry? You should be careful not to break your leg again.

Daniel: I know, but I have an appointment in the Student Union at four o'clock.

Cindy: Is that why you were walking so fast?

Daniel: Yeah, it's in a few minutes, and this is only the cafeteria.

Cindy: Well, you should slow down now and rest your leg a little.

Daniel: Alright, I should let my friends know that I'll be late.

Cindy: Send a text message immediately. Then let's go to see a doctor.

Daniel: OK, thanks for the help.

Vocabulary

Unit 01

colleague
acquaintance
boss
relative
classmate
neighbor

volunteer work
healthier
increase
chance
mental health
surely
issue

Unit 02

birthday
Valentine's Day
Easter
St. Patrick's Day
wedding anniversary
Christmas
Parents' Day
Groundhog Day
Thanksgiving Day
New Year's Day
Halloween

celebrate
tradition
superstition
predict
forecast
Virgin Mary
hedgehog

Unit 03

go on a picnic
plant trees
go surfing
go water-skiing
fly a kite
go sunbathing
pick fruit
build a snowman
go snowboarding

the latest
the brightest
the biggest
the hottest
the happiest
the earliest
the most expensive
the most unusual
the best
the worst
the farthest

snowbirds
flea market
sellers
move
warm
climate
vacation places

Unit 04

subway
sports car
SUV
limousine
van
express bus
maglev train
ferry

train
airplane
snowstorm
cancel
flights
tickets
station

cruise ship
go through security
weight restriction
expense

Unit 05

celery
cabbage
wheat
oats
plum
beef
salmon
nuts
olive oil

phytochemicals
grains
stuffed
spinach
boneless
skinless
halves

teaspoon
black pepper
basil
powdered
frozen
melted
squeezed
dry
roasted
low–fat
whole-wheat
crumbs
season
red pepper
dip
coat
baking sheet
remove
toothpicks
serve

Unit 06

tow truck
pile-up
hit and run
T-bone
head-on collision
bump each other

fender-bender
fatality

speeding ticket
traffic jam
car scratch
proof

insurance
KPH zone

Unit 07

twice a month
never
every few hours
once a year
several times
a week
frequently
all the time
from time to time
rarely

hardly ever
seldom
occasionally
usually
normally
generally

habit
set
priorities
maintaining
responsible
lifestyle
renew

Unit 08

boarding pass
economy class
business class
passport
luggage
aisle seat
window seat
arrival and departure

security checkpoint
customs officer
airline ticket
exit row seat
overhead bins
suitcase
check in
waive
baggage fee

Unit 09

vegan option
today's special
beverage
starter
menu
main dish
reservation
side dish
dessert
cutlery
starters
dessert
beverage
pay for
order
recommend
vegetarian
serve
terrace
charge
trays

Unit 10

stomachache
prescription
medicine
nauseous
broken leg

headache
fever
exhausted
be scared of
sick
injections
pain
suffer from
throw up
use up
get well

must
have to
should
ought to

uncomfortable
sore muscles
unclear
vision
dizziness
dry eyes
syndrome
physical therapy

Unit 11

reply
text message
email address
attachment
BCC (blind carbon copy)
CC (carbon copy)
messenger
emoticon
delete
spam
appointment
unprofessional
edit

postal mail
telephone call
mobile phone call
fax
instant messenger
delivery service
turn off
respond
silent mode
Internet shorthand

Unit 12

auditorium
library
laboratory
Student Union
dormitory
College of Engineering
campus
theater
cafeteria

administration building
Chemistry department
campus tour
surrounding
explore
visitor
depart

how often
how long
how far
how high